Read Better to Write Better

Tatsuaki Tomioka
James Hill

KINSEIDO

Kinseido Publishing Co., Ltd.
3-21 Kanda Jimbo-cho, Chiyoda-ku,
Tokyo 101-0051, Japan

Copyright © 2002 by Tatsuaki Tomioka
and James Hill

All rights reserved. No part of this publication may be reproduced, stored in a retrieval system, or transmitted, in any form or by any means, electronic, mechanical, photocopying, recording or otherwise, without the prior permission of the publisher.

First published 2002 by Kinseido Publishing Co., Ltd.

写真提供
P. 15, 28, 32, 59, 78, 82, 毎日新聞社

はしがき

本書のねらいは次の4点です。

1. 第一義的には、英語の基礎的ライティング能力を養成すること。
2. モデル英文を付け、その音声CDを作成することにより、リーディング教材、リスニング教材の側面も併せ持つ、総合英語教材としての性格を、特徴として有すること。
3. 各ユニットが、トピックと広義の文構造（文法、語法を含む）の新たな組み合わせを具現した、テキストとして統一性の高いものであること。それにより、各ユニットの到達目標を明確にし、いわゆる絞りのきいた授業、効率的な学習を可能にすること。
4. エクササイズと解説をなるべく有機的に関連付け、学習者が利用しやすいレイアウトを心がけること。

以下、上記のねらいについてそれぞれ説明します。

1について

日本の大学生の一般的状況としては、中学高校で、ライティングの指導があまりなされないままの状態で大学に入ってくる場合が多いようです。いわゆる受験のための文法、語法、熟語などは断片的に知ってはいますが、それらは、志望校に合格するために当面の課題であった、入試でよく出される、カッコ穴埋めや、並べ替えの文法、語法、熟語問題に対処するための知識であり、発信とか実際の活用というレベルとはあまり関連性のないもの、というのが大方の実情ではないかと考えられます。

そこで、中学高校で習ってきた構文知識を基礎にして、身近な話題を中心として、実際に使える基本的なライティング能力の養成に役立つテキストを作る、というのが本書を作成するうえでの大きなねらいとなっています。

2について

本書を作成するにあたって最も工夫を要したところは、モデル英文の執筆です。これはnative speakerと念入りな検討を交えながら作成したオリジナル英文です。このモデル英文作成にあたっては以下の点に留意しました。

a. 学習者にとって文字通り、ライティングのためのモデルとするに足る内容と形式を備えていること。学習者が暗誦するに足る、模範的英文作成を心がける。トピックの選択については、大学生にとって身近なもの、全体的には、現代日本人の（特に若者の）ものの考え方・感じ方と現代の日本事情の一端を外に向けて発信する、という内容を中心とする。

b. モデル英文のバラエティを持たせるために、3種類の異なったスタイルの英文（三人称のエッセイ、一人称の物語的文章、対話文）を用いる。
c. モデル英文を録音した音声CDを付属することで、リスニング用英文としても活用できるようにする。
d. 学習者に、単なる読み流し、聞き流しをさせず、モデル英文を消化吸収させるために、いわゆる'復文'の手法を一部取り入れる。即ち、モデル英文のkey clausesの日本語訳例をテキストで与えておき、「オリジナル英文→訳文→オリジナル英文」の演習を授業担当の先生、または学習者が必要に応じて適宜行えるようにする。

3について

　言うまでもなく、ライティングには「何について書くか」というトピック性（例：学生生活、高齢化社会、日本人のものの考え方、etc.）の問題と、「どういう語句を使ってどういう構文で書くか」という、表現語彙や文構造的テーマ（例：口語体か文語体などの文体的な特徴、仮主語もしくは具体主語（名詞句）を用いた構文、無生物主語構文、etc.）の問題があります。学ぶ側にとっての学習効率という観点からはこの両者がうまくかみ合っていることが望ましいということは自明のことであろうと思います。そこで各ユニットで学習の焦点となる文法・構文上のテーマを設定しました（例：Unit 3——仮定法）。

4について

　構文に関してのkey clausesについては、学習者の参考になるよう、文法・構文的'価値判断'を「表現のポイント」という形で付けました。「表現のポイント」は学習者が極力読んでくれるように、簡略で平明な記述を心がけたつもりです。文法語法解説はまとめて書いてしまうといわゆる解説のための解説になってしまい、読者にとってプレッシャーになりがちですので、小出しにして、演習問題と一体化するレイアウトにしました。

　学生の皆さんが、このテキストの学習を通して、リスニング、リーディングを含めた英語の総合力が上がり、それによって作文・会話などの、英語の発信力が向上すれば、筆者の意図は達せられたといえます。最後にこのテキストの英文全体をチェックしていただき、数々の有益なアドバイス、コメントを頂いたJames Hill氏に心から感謝の意を表します。

2002年1月

富岡 龍明

本書の利用の仕方

1．まず付属CDで当該ユニットのモデル英文を、本文を見ずに数回繰り返して聞く。
2．次に、モデル英文を数回、音読する（黙読ではなく音読することが大切）。その際 key clausesになっているところは特に注意を払って読む。
3．わからない単語・語句などの意味、用法を辞書で確認する。
4．モデル英文がだいたい頭に入ったら（少なくともkey clausesが口をついて出てくるまでになっている必要がある）、KEY CLAUSES の演習をやってみる。ここでは訳例として与えられている日本文から元の英文を組み立ててみる作業を行なう。この作業を通じて、一層深くkey clausesが習得できる。
5．語彙の確認作業として WORDS & PHRASES をやってみる。
6．EXERCISES の和文英訳をやってみる。ある程度ヒントが与えられているので、モデル英文を参照しながら、自分なりの英文を組み立ててみる。なるべく辞書などに頼らず書いてみること。
7．ゆとりがあれば*LET'S TRY!*をやってみる。

以上はあくまで本書の使い方の一例です。実際にはこのテキストを使って授業される先生の指示に従ってください。

● 付属CDについて
　巻末に付属しているCDには、本書のモデル英文が全て収録されています。なお、CDの頭出し番号は、各ユニットの番号に対応しています。

TABLE OF CONTENTS

UNIT 1 *What makes college students work part-time?* — 8
大学生のアルバイト
◆非人称主語（impersonal subjects）を使った構文（1）

UNIT 2 *Staying healthy—a Japanese obsession* — 12
健康志向国民
◆非人称主語（impersonal subjects）を使った構文（2）

UNIT 3 *How I wish I were at my first-choice college!* — 16
当世大学生気質
◆仮定法

UNIT 4 *Staying with a family abroad* — 20
心配なホームステイ
◆発話動詞（say, tell, talk, speak）

UNIT 5 *Japan and America* — 25
日本人にとってアメリカとは
◆否定詞

UNIT 6 *Drinking as part of youth culture* — 29
酒と大学生
◆形容詞構文（1）

UNIT 7 *I don't belong here* — 33
帰国子女のカルチャーショック
◆形容詞構文（2）

UNIT 8 *What's the purpose of work?* — 37
働きがいとは何か？
◆名詞構文

UNIT 9 *The Japanese as half-Asian* — 41
アジア VS. 日本
◆時制——過去と過去完了

UNIT 10 *Why few Japanese can speak English* — 45
なぜ英語が話せない？
◆接続詞

UNIT 11 *How I wish I could live on my own!* — 49
当世親子関係
◆助動詞

UNIT 12	*The pros and cons of so-called 'exam English'* 受験英語の功罪 ◆感覚・認識動詞	54
UNIT 13	*An aging society* 高齢化社会の行く末 ◆比較級（1）	59
UNIT 14	*Do we have to live in a polluted environment?* 不便に耐えよう──環境問題 ◆比較級（2）	63
UNIT 15	*My view of marriage* 結婚はちょっと ◆代名詞	66
UNIT 16	*Is Japan an international society?* 日本の「国際度」は？ ◆進行形	71
UNIT 17	*Job prospects for college students* 大学生の就職難 ◆文修飾副詞	75
UNIT 18	*A problem with Japan's education system* 勉強はあとから──教育問題 ◆'when'の2つの用法	79
UNIT 19	*High school vs. cram school* 塾か学校か？ ◆使役動詞	83
UNIT 20	*Why are cars so important?* 車がそんなに大切？ ◆総合演習	88

UNIT 1
What makes college students work part-time?

◆非人称主語 (impersonal subjects) を使った構文 (1)

MODEL PASSAGE　*third-person essay*

以下の文章をCDで聴いてみましょう。また①～⑥の英文に注意しながら, 繰り返し音読してみましょう。

　A lot of young Japanese work part-time while they are at college. Waiter (or waitress), shop assistant, and private teacher—these are some of the typical jobs they take. Take Miyuki, a girl student who is working part-time at a discount store. If you asked her ①**what made her decide to take the job**, she'd say she just wanted to earn some pocket money for herself. Her parents are paying her college fees, and ②**this means that she doesn't have to work her way through college**. For most parents, ③**sending children to college is a big financial burden**, while for the students, ④**going to college can be a decision that guarantees them some of the most carefree days of their life**.

　For students whose parents can't support them, it can be hard: work or starve. An exaggeration? Well, perhaps. But even for those who aren't forced to work, ⑤**earning money can be very tough, even traumatic**.

　"Things aren't as easy as you might think", the female student would say, "⑥**Doing this job means having to put up with my boss all day**—and he's probably the most demanding person on the planet." At least her job should teach her that life is never easy.

KEY CLAUSES

以下の日本語は，MODEL PASSAGEの重要構文①〜⑥の和訳です。本文を見ずに，この日本語から元の英文を作り上げる練習をしてみましょう。

① どうして彼女が今の仕事をする気になったのか。

② これはつまり，彼女は自分で働いて学資を出して大学を卒業する必要がない，ということなのです。

③ 子供を大学にやるということは大変な経済的負担です。

④ 大学に行くということは学生達に，人生のうちでもっとも気楽な日々を保証してくれる選択（決定）なのです。

⑤ お金を稼ぐというのはとてもきびしい，場合によっては精神的にあとをひくものなのです。

⑥ この仕事をするということは，私の上司に対していつも我慢してなきゃいけない，ということなのです。

WORDS & PHRASES

次の日本語の意味に相当する英語を，MODEL PASSAGEの中から抜き出し，書き取ってみましょう。

1. バイトをする　　　　　＿＿＿＿＿＿＿＿＿＿＿＿＿＿
2. 店員　　　　　　　　　＿＿＿＿＿＿＿＿＿＿＿＿＿＿
3. 家庭教師　　　　　　　＿＿＿＿＿＿＿＿＿＿＿＿＿＿
4. 大学の授業料　　　　　＿＿＿＿＿＿＿＿＿＿＿＿＿＿
5. 経済的負担　　　　　　＿＿＿＿＿＿＿＿＿＿＿＿＿＿
6. 気楽な　　　　　　　　＿＿＿＿＿＿＿＿＿＿＿＿＿＿
7. 誇張　　　　　　　　　＿＿＿＿＿＿＿＿＿＿＿＿＿＿
8. 心に傷を残すような　　＿＿＿＿＿＿＿＿＿＿＿＿＿＿
9. 要求がきびしい　　　　＿＿＿＿＿＿＿＿＿＿＿＿＿＿
10. 我慢する　　　　　　　＿＿＿＿＿＿＿＿＿＿＿＿＿＿

EXERCISES

次の日本語の文を英語に直しなさい。

> 表現のポイント ☞①
> タイトルの英文と①の英文のように，whatの次に，make＋目的語＋原形動詞（または形容詞）の形で，日本語で直訳すれば「何が～を～させたか」となるようなstructureが英語ではよく用いられる。

1. 「ぼくはこのバイトに向いてないよ。」「どうして君はそう考えるんだい。」
   ▶「～に向いていない」be not cut out for～

2. 「どうして今のバイトをやめようと決心したの。」「給料が安すぎるからですよ。」
   ▶「やめる」quit

3. 「どうしてあなたは家庭教師という仕事に興味を持つようになったのですか。」「他のパートに比べて結構お金になるからです。」
   ▶「家庭教師という仕事」private teaching (or teaching someone privately)

> 表現のポイント ☞②, ⑥
> A means B「AはBを意味する」のstructureでも，人称主語をとるのと同様（例：I mean it「俺は本気で言ってるんだ。」），Aの項目としてthis, that, あるいは動詞の～ing形などの非人称主語をとることが珍しくない。このstructureでBの部分は，名詞相当語句（動詞の～ing形，to不定詞も含む）やthat節がくる。

4. 学生であるということは必ずしもヒマだということじゃありません。実際思ったよりずっと忙しいです。
   ▶「大学生であるということ」being a college (university) student

5. バイトで忙しいということは勉強する時間があまり取れないということなんです。
   ▶「バイトで忙しいということ」being busy with a part-time job

6. このラーメン屋は人使いが荒いから，ここで働くとドット老けるって感じだな。
   ▶「ラーメン屋」noodle shop 「人使いが荒い」ここでの仕事(job)は(demanding)と考える。

表現のポイント　☞③，④，⑤
例えば，「大学に通うのは金がかかる」を英語で表す時，It is expensive to go to collegeのように，いわゆる仮のitを主語として書くこともできるが，Going to college is expensiveのように，具体的に主語を書き表すこともできる（こちらの方が語数も少なくより簡潔）。その場合To go to college...のように，to不定詞を使うよりも，〜ingのほうが一般的。

7. 夕方の5時から夜中の2時まで働くのがつらくなってきたよ。このまま続けると体をこわすような気がする。
　▶「夜中」am もしくは in the morning 「つらくなってくる」はbe beginning to tell on someoneなどが使える。「体をこわす」病気になると考える。

8. 自分で稼いで生活する，というのがずいぶん以前からやってみたかったことなんです。やってみると意外におもしろいものです。
　▶「自分で稼いで生活する」living on my own 「ずいぶん〜ことなんです」関係詞のwhatを使う。「ずいぶん以前から」for years

―― LET'S TRY! ――

A 'What makes (made) someone V?' の構文を使って10 words以上の英文を書いてみましょう。

B '〜ing means (meant) 〜ing' の構文を使って15 words以上の英文を書いてみましょう。

UNIT 1

UNIT 2
Staying healthy—a Japanese obsession

◆非人称主語（impersonal subjects）を使った構文（2）

MODEL PASSAGE　*third-person essay*

以下の文章をCDで聴いてみましょう。また①〜④の英文に注意しながら，繰り返し音読してみましょう。

　①**A glance at the food section of any supermarket in Japan will show you how keen the Japanese are to stay healthy.** There are piles of health-improving foodstuffs like additive-free, preservative-free *tofu*, *natto* (fermented soybeans), and pickled vegetables. They sell in huge quantities. And drugstores offer a great variety of semi-medicinal drinks, which are supposed to give temporary relief from fatigue. Office workers often drink them before or after a hard day's work, or students before taking exams.

　②**And these days, mail-order enables customers to get almost any kind of health food.** The variety is virtually limitless—ranging from magical mushrooms to shark's cartilage. ③**Foods like these help the Japanese to achieve the longest life span in the world.**

　There is one other important fact about the health-oriented Japanese lifestyle. ④**A little observation of their eating habits will reveal how carefully they avoid fatty food.** For most Japanese being healthy is associated with being slim and slender. Their view—a strongly-held one—is that fat shortens one's life. There are quite a few TV programs and magazines telling people how to reduce their body-fat. For many Japanese, eating fat-free food for the sake of a long life is almost an obsession.

KEY CLAUSES

以下の日本語は，MODEL PASSAGEの重要構文①〜④の和訳です。本文を見ずに，この日本語から元の英文を作り上げる練習をしてみましょう。

① 日本のスーパーの食料品コーナーをのぞくと日本人が健康を保ちたいと願う気持ちの強さがわかります。

② そして最近では通信販売でほとんどの健康食品が手に入るようになりました。

③ こういった食品は日本人の寿命を世界最長にするのに役立っているのです。

④ 日本人の食生活をちょっと観察しただけで彼らが脂肪分の多い食品を慎重に避けているということがわかります。

WORDS & PHRASES

次の日本語の意味に相当する英語を，MODEL PASSAGEの中から抜き出し，書き取ってみましょう。

1. 食料品コーナー　＿＿＿＿＿＿＿＿＿＿＿＿＿＿＿
2. 健康を保つ　＿＿＿＿＿＿＿＿＿＿＿＿＿＿＿
3. 無添加の　＿＿＿＿＿＿＿＿＿＿＿＿＿＿＿
4. 保存料を使っていない　＿＿＿＿＿＿＿＿＿＿＿＿＿＿＿
5. 健康ドリンク　＿＿＿＿＿＿＿＿＿＿＿＿＿＿＿
6. 健康食品　＿＿＿＿＿＿＿＿＿＿＿＿＿＿＿
7. 通信販売　＿＿＿＿＿＿＿＿＿＿＿＿＿＿＿
8. 寿命　＿＿＿＿＿＿＿＿＿＿＿＿＿＿＿
9. 食生活　＿＿＿＿＿＿＿＿＿＿＿＿＿＿＿
10. こだわり　＿＿＿＿＿＿＿＿＿＿＿＿＿＿＿

EXERCISES

次の日本語の文を英語に直しなさい。

> 表現のポイント　☞①, ④
> 「～をちょっと見れば（～をすこし観察すれば）～であることがわかる」などの日本語表現はglance, observationなどの名詞を主語として, show, revealなどの動詞を組み合わせることで, 英語らしい無生物主語構文が出来上がる。

1. ちょっと新聞の広告欄をみただけで, 健康食品が今どれほどブームかがわかる。
    ▶「新聞の広告欄」newspaper ads　「ブーム」popular

2. 日本人の食生活をちょっと観察しただけで, 今どれほど外食が多くなっているかがわかる。
    ▶「外食が多い」頻繁に外で食べる（eat out）と考える。

3. あるアンケート調査によると, 10代の肥満がここ10年で急増しているとのことだ。明らかに日本人の食生活の欧米化が原因の一つだ。
    ▶「アンケート調査」survey　「10代の肥満」fat teenagers　「欧米化する」westernize

> 表現のポイント　☞②, ③
> 「XのおかげでYがZをすることが可能になった」という構文はX enables Y to do Zの形で表すことができる。同じように, 「Xは, YがZをすることに役立つ」という意味合いならばX helps Y (to) do Zの構文が使える。

4. このマシーンを使えば家の中で毎日適度の運動ができます。もうわざわざ外で運動する必要はありません。
    ▶「～が～を可能にする」と考えてenableを使う。「適度の運動をする」do some exercise

5. インターネットを使えば自分が欲しいと思うどんな健康食品でも簡単に手に入る。全くインターネットは便利なものだ。
    ▶「インターネット」the Internet　「簡単に」easily (with ease)

6. こういった新しい器具は寝たきりのお年寄りが快適な暮らしをするのに役立つだろう。これからはこの種の器具がどんどん出回ることになるだろう。
   ▶「器具」device 「寝たきりのお年寄り」bed-ridden elderly people 「快適な」comfortable

7. 日本人には，健康維持に役立つことならなんでも積極的にやってみるという人が多くいます。だから年の割に元気な人が多いのかもしれません。
   ▶「健康を維持する」stay healthy 「年の割に」for one's age

LET'S TRY!

A ③と同じ用法の 'help' を使って10 words以上の英文を書いてみましょう。

B 'Bad effects of eating fast food very frequently' というタイトルで100 words程度の英文を書いてみましょう。

UNIT 3

How I wish I were at my first-choice college!

◆仮定法

MODEL PASSAGE　*first-person narrative*

以下の文章をCDで聴いてみましょう。また，①〜⑤の英文に注意しながら繰り返し音読してみましょう。

Kenji is in his first year at university in Kyoto. He's majoring in English. He enjoys university life on the whole, but he can't forget that his university wasn't his first choice. He sometimes wonders if it would be better to stop studying at this university and try again to get into the one he'd always wanted to go to.

　What a day! I got a real telling-off from Professor Higgins in his oral English class today. ①**I should have known better than to be in class with my mobile phone on.** A beeping sound from somewhere, getting louder. Oh, no! It's me! My phone! At last it's off. But it was too late. Professor Higgins was glaring at me. His look said, "You idiot!" ②**Only someone who has been glared at by a T.Rex would understand how I felt at that moment.** "Kenji!", roared the T.Rex, "You've done it again! If that happens once more, you're finished; I'll mark you zero in the end-of-term exam. Do you understand?" This was only a sample of what he threw at me in class. Professor Higgins is a very keen teacher; he prepares carefully, and teaches well, but he is perhaps too sensitive to interruptions.

　That's the kind of thing that happens to me here. To be honest, I'm not really happy the way things are. ③**I sometimes wonder what life would have been like if I'd managed to get a place at Keihoku University in Tokyo, which was my first choice.** ④**If I'd been successful, my parents would be a lot happier, and I would be, too.** Wouldn't it be better if I left and tried Keihoku University again next year? No, it would be torture to have to do all that exam preparation again. I'll stay in Kyoto. I like everything about this old city, except that prices are a bit too high.

What I need to do is make the best of my life here. I must try to make my life better, more enjoyable—I need a fresh start. Perhaps I could dye my hair. Light brown would be a good colour. ⑤**Dyeing my hair was the last thing I felt like doing when I was at high school.** But now that so many of the students here are getting their hair dyed, I'd feel left out if I didn't do the same.

KEY CLAUSES

以下の日本語は，MODEL PASSAGEの重要構文①〜⑤の和訳です。本文を見ずに，この日本語から元の英文を作り上げる練習をしてみましょう。

① 携帯のスイッチをいれたまま授業に出たのはまずかった。

② ティラノサウルスににらまれたことのある人だけがそのときの僕の気持ちがわかるだろう。

③ 第一志望だった東京の京北大学に何とか入れていたらどうなっていたろうと時々思うことがある。

④ もし受かっていたら，両親も今ごろはもっと喜んでいるに違いないし，僕も同じ気持ちだろう。

⑤ 髪を染めるなんてことは高校の時は全然やりたいなんて思わなかった。

WORDS & PHRASES

次の日本語の意味に相当する英語を，MODEL PASSAGEの中から抜き出し，書き取ってみましょう。

1. 〜を専攻する　　　　＿＿＿＿＿＿＿＿＿＿＿＿＿＿＿＿＿
2. 英会話クラス　　　　＿＿＿＿＿＿＿＿＿＿＿＿＿＿＿＿＿
3. 〜をにらみつける　　＿＿＿＿＿＿＿＿＿＿＿＿＿＿＿＿＿
4. 熱心な先生　　　　　＿＿＿＿＿＿＿＿＿＿＿＿＿＿＿＿＿
5. 携帯電話　　　　　　＿＿＿＿＿＿＿＿＿＿＿＿＿＿＿＿＿
6. 期末試験　　　　　　＿＿＿＿＿＿＿＿＿＿＿＿＿＿＿＿＿
7. 妨害　　　　　　　　＿＿＿＿＿＿＿＿＿＿＿＿＿＿＿＿＿
8. 拷問　　　　　　　　＿＿＿＿＿＿＿＿＿＿＿＿＿＿＿＿＿
9. 心機一転　　　　　　＿＿＿＿＿＿＿＿＿＿＿＿＿＿＿＿＿
10. （自分の）髪を染める　＿＿＿＿＿＿＿＿＿＿＿＿＿＿＿＿＿

EXERCISES

次の日本語の文を英語に直しなさい。

> 表現のポイント ☞①
> 日本語の「～したのはよくなかった，～したのは良識がなかった」などの表現は，直訳的には「～をするよりももっと分別があるべきだった」の意味を表すshould have known better than to Vの形で表すことができる。また，時制を変えてshould know better than to Vで「～するのはよくない，～するのは良識がない」などの意味を表すことができる。

1. Underwood先生の英語の時間に居眠りしていたのはまずかった。今度やったら単位がもらえないかもしれない。
   ▶「居眠りする」doze 「単位」credit

2. そこの君！授業中にものを食べるのは非常識ですよ。教室はものを学ぶところです。ものを食べるところではありません。
   ▶「～するのは非常識だ」should know better than to V（1と比較して時制に注意）

> 表現のポイント ☞②
> 英語の仮定法の用法の一つに誇張法があげられる。例えば本文②のように，架空の，もしくは極端なことがらを仮定的にひきあいにだすことで，ある具体的状況での，「にらむ」という行為の'凄み'を際立たせることができる。

3. おそらくサハラ砂漠で迷子になったことのある人だけがその時の私の心細さを理解できるでしょう。
   ▶「サハラ砂漠」the Sahara 「迷子になる」be (get) lost 「心細い」helpless

> 表現のポイント ☞③，④
> 仮定法の過去完了用法は帰結節では主語＋助動詞＋have＋過去分詞，ifをつかった従属節ではif主語＋had＋過去分詞の形式をとり，すでに発生した事実とは異なる，過去の可能性に言及する働きを示す。④のように，If節では仮定法過去完了であっても，帰結節では仮定法過去となって，現在の事実と異なる，ひとつの可能な事態を表すことがある。

4. もしわたしが家を出て一人暮らしをしていたらどんな風になっていただろうかと思うことが時々ある。
    ▶「家を出て一人暮らしをする」leave home to live on my own

5. もし私が受かっていなかったら，大学受験そのものをあきらめていたかもしれない。そして今ごろはとても落ち込んでいることだろう。
    ▶「受かっていない」be unsuccessful 「落ち込む」be depressed

> 表現のポイント ₿⑤
> X is the last thing S+Vの形で，「Xは考えてもいない，全く思いもよらない事柄である」といった意味を表す。

6. 東京で暮らすなんてことは去年まではやってみようとも思わなかったことだ。昨年東京支社に移ることになって，今東京での生活はとても楽しい。
    ▶全体の構文をX was the last thing S+Vにする。「東京支社」the Tokyo branch

7. 海外で就職するなんてことは全く考えてもいません。外国には旅行では行きたいと思うけど，住みたいとは思いません。
    ▶全体の構文をX is the last thing S+Vにする。「海外で就職する」get a job abroad

---

LET'S TRY!

A 'should have known better than to V' の構文を使って15 words以上の英文を書いてみましょう。

B 'X is (was) the last thing S+V' の構文を使って15 words以上の英文を書いてみ

UNIT 3

UNIT 4

Staying with a family abroad

◆発話動詞（say, tell, talk, speak）

MODEL PASSAGE *dialogue*

以下の文章をCDで聴いてみましょう。また①〜⑤の英文に注意しながら，繰り返し音読してみましょう。

Naomi is in her second year at a women's college in Fukuoka. This summer she is going to Los Angeles to stay with a family there for one month. She is very excited about visiting the second largest city in the U.S. But at the same time she has some worries because she has never been abroad. So she talks to Professor Fowler about her worries. Professor Fowler has taken groups of students to Los Angeles several times, so he knows a lot about what it is like for Japanese students to spend time there.

Prof. Fowler: ①**Naomi, you say that you're worried about the small children in your host family.**

Naomi: Yes, a little bit. They have two children: a 4-year-old boy and a 6-year-old girl. As a matter of fact, I'm not used to dealing with small children.

Prof. Fowler: Well, if you want to improve your English, getting to know those young kids could be very helpful; ②**it'd be very good for you to get used to the way they talk.**

Naomi: I'm afraid I won't be able to catch what they say, because children often don't speak clearly. And then communication will break down, and I'll have a hard time while I'm staying with them. That's one of the things I'm worried about.

Prof. Fowler: Naomi, communication involves a number of different aspects. Attitude, for example, is a very important one, and it's sometimes more important than the talk itself. ③**Be nice and friendly when you talk to the children,** and there shouldn't be any communication problems.

Naomi: I know what you mean, but in the photo the family sent me they look very naughty. One of my friends had a lot of trouble with the children in her host family when she went to Los Angeles last year.

④**She told me the two children, a 3-year-old boy and a 5-year-old girl, were very noisy and selfish, and they kept bothering her all the time,** so she didn't have enough time to study while she was there.

Prof. Fowler: She was unlucky. From experience, I can assure you that nine out of ten Japanese students are wholly satisfied with their home stay experience abroad.

Naomi: I hope I won't be one of the unlucky 10 per cent. Actually, Professor Fowler, I have another worry. I'll be the only person staying with my host family. I thought being alone would give me more chance to talk to them. ⑤**But I might just as well have chosen to be with someone else who speaks Japanese,** because then I'd be able to get help when I had a problem.

Prof. Fowler: I think you've made the right choice. Being alone in an unfamiliar environment may make you feel uneasy at first, but it won't be long before you get used to it, and I understand your host parents are both experienced teachers. They should know how to help you when you have difficulties. Anyway, you'll find it's a great advantage to be exposed to 'real English' all the time without any help from people speaking your own language.

Naomi: I hope so.

Prof. Fowler: Naomi, don't worry. You'll be OK. If you were with someone from Japan, you might depend on him or her too much, or vice versa. That means you'd end up using Japanese far too often. In many cases, when two Japanese students are staying with a family overseas, they tend to talk to each other in Japanese all the time, and don't get close to the family. That makes everyone involved very unhappy.

Naomi: I see your point, Professor Fowler. It's been very nice talking to you. Thanks very much for all your helpful advice.

Prof. Fowler: You're welcome. Naomi. I hope you have a nice trip.

KEY CLAUSES

以下の日本語は，MODEL PASSAGEの重要構文①〜⑤の和訳です。本文を見ずに，この日本語から元の英文を作り上げる練習をしてみましょう。

① 直美，君はホストファミリーの小さな子供達のことが気になるというんだね。

② そこの子供の話し方に慣れるのは君にとってとてもいいことなんじゃないか。

③ そこの子供と話す時にはやさしく，あたたかく接しなさい。

④ 彼女から聞いたのですが，その3歳の男の子と，5歳の女の子がとってもうるさくて，わがままで，彼女をいつも困らせていたのです。

⑤ しかし，日本語をしゃべる人と一緒でもよかったかもしれません。そちらの方が困った時には助けてもらえるから。

WORDS & PHRASES

次の日本語の意味に相当する英語を，MODEL PASSAGEの中から抜き出し，書き取ってみましょう。

1. 女子大 _____
2. 態度 _____
3. 腕白な _____
4. わがままな _____
5. 断言する _____
6. 正しい選択 _____
7. 不慣れな環境 _____
8. ベテラン教師 _____
9. 利点 _____
10. 逆 _____

EXERCISES

次の日本語の文を英語に直しなさい。

> 表現のポイント　☞①
> sayはtellと同様，発話内容の伝達に重点があるため，名詞句や節（主語＋述語）などの目的語を従える。

1. その旅行業者は，シアトルの四週間のホームステイで40万くらいだといっています。
   ▶「旅行業者」travel agency

2. 坂本君に言わせると，ホームステイするならイギリスの田舎に限る，ということだ。
   ▶「田舎」countryside

> 表現のポイント　☞②，③
> talkはspeakと同様，発話の内容よりも，しゃべるという行為に意味の重点がある。そのため，そのあとに名詞句や節などを目的語として従えることはない。

3. 最近の学生は授業中あまりおしゃべりはしなくなったが，その代わりせっせと携帯でメールのやりとりをしているのが多い。
   ▶「携帯」cellular (mobile) phone

4. 私は去年ロンドンにホームステイしましたが，その家はずいぶん客の多い家で，おかげでいろんな人達といろんなことを話せて，英会話力がつきました。

> 表現のポイント　☞④
> tellはsayと同様，伝達内容重視型の動詞だが，tellはsayと異なり，内容を誰に伝えるか，つまり間接目的語の部分が必須である点に注意。(tell the truth, tell a lieなどは例外的用法。)

5. James先生，先生が昨年ひとりで北欧を回られた時の体験談をもっと私達に聞かせてください。
   ▶「北欧」northern Europe

UNIT 4

6. 私がある人から聞いた話では，日本人学生のなかには極端に無口なのがけっこういるので，あまり日本人学生を引き受けたがらないホストファミリーもあるということだ。
   ▶ 「極端に無口な」extremely quiet

> **表現のポイント** ☞ ⑤
> speakはtalkと同様，発話行為そのものに意味の重点がある。したがって名詞句や，節などの目的語を取らない点に注意。（ただしspeak Englishなどは例外的用法）

7. Taylor先生は，英語をしゃべる時にはいちいち間違いを気にしなくていいよ，と授業中私達に言うけれど，やっぱり間違いは気になるものだよ。
   ▶ 「授業中」in class

LET'S TRY !

A 動詞 'talk' をつかって10 words以上の英文を書いてみましょう。

B 'The country I'd most like to visit' というタイトルで100 words程度の英文を書いてみましょう。

Japan and America

UNIT 5

◆否定詞

MODEL PASSAGE *third-person essay*

以下の文章をCDで聴いてみましょう。また，①〜⑤の英文に注意しながら繰り返し音読してみましょう。

To the Japanese, the United States of America is a special country. Historically, it was the Americans that, in 1854, put an end to the long-standing political isolation of Japan. They were just like trigger-happy cowboys kicking open a locked door and shouting, "All we want is a business relationship with you; we mean no harm." America defeated the samurai country through gunboat diplomacy. ①**Japan had never before been through such a shameful experience.** America defeated Japan again in 1945. Japan fought against more than 40 countries in World War II, but many Japanese feel that the most formidable enemy, the one chiefly responsible for their surrender, was the United States.

②**When the Japanese realized that their samurai spiritualism had little chance of competing with American rationalism based on science and technology, they became the most eager students of the American way.** ③**There were very few American things that escaped the attention of the Japanese**—Hollywood movies, American pop culture, hi-tech industries, Coca-Cola, McDonald's hamburgers, were all put under the microscope. For the average Japanese, America was, is, and will remain a yardstick by which to measure how civilized Japan is. This is reflected in a general tendency on the part of the Japanese mass media to compare their own country with America whenever they discuss something, with comments like "In this, Japan lags far behind the United States." Japan pays perhaps ten times as much attention to the United States as the United States does to Japan. Things may be changing a little bit these days, now that Japanese things such as *sushi*, *teriyaki* and Honda cars are becoming more popular in the US, ④**but the traditional Japan-US relationship itself is unlikely to change**; for many Japanese, America will remain one of the few countries they look up to.

KEY CLAUSES

以下の日本語は，MODEL PASSAGEの重要構文①〜④の和訳です。本文を見ずに，この日本語から元の英文を作り上げる練習をしてみましょう。

① 日本はそれまでそういう屈辱的な経験をしたことがなかった。

② 日本人は彼らの武士道的精神主義が，アメリカ的な，科学技術に基づく合理主義に対してほとんど歯が立たないとわかった時，アメリカ的なものを学ぶもっとも熱心な生徒になった。

③ アメリカの文物で日本人の関心の対象にならなかったものはほとんどなかった。

④ しかし伝統的な日米間関係そのものが変わる可能性はほとんどない。

WORDS & PHRASES

次の日本語の意味に相当する英語を，MODEL PASSAGEの中から抜き出し，書き取ってみましょう。

1. 政治的孤立（鎖国体制） _____
2. 通商関係 _____
3. 砲艦外交 _____
4. 強敵 _____
5. 精神主義 _____
6. 合理主義 _____
7. 大衆文化 _____
8. ハイテク産業 _____
9. ものさし _____
10. マスコミ _____

EXERCISES

次の日本語の文を英語に直しなさい。

> 表現のポイント ☞①
> 現在完了形，もしくは過去完了形と否定詞neverを組み合わせることで，現在まで，もしくは過去のある時点まで，ある事柄が一度も発生しなかった，というような，経験の全否定を表すことができる。

1. 第2次大戦に敗れるまで日本は他国に国土を占領されたことは一度もなかった。
   ▶「占領する」occupy

2. 建国以来アメリカは他国の侵略を受けたことは一度もない。その点で，頻繁に外国の侵略にさらされてきたヨーロッパの国々とずいぶん異なっている。
   ▶「建国以来」since its foundation 「その点で」in this (or in this respect)

> 表現のポイント ☞②
> chance, understanding, knowledgeなどの非可算名詞とlittleを組み合わせることで，量的な意味で，ほとんど〜ないという否定の意味を表すことができる。

3. 戦前は，入手できる情報が非常に少なかったため，アメリカの合理主義がどのようなものかについて日本人はほとんど理解していなかった。
   ▶「〜がどのようなものか」what X is like

4. 日本が，アメリカの圧倒的な軍事力に到底太刀打ちできないとわかったのは実際にアメリカと戦いはじめてからだった。
   ▶「圧倒的な軍事力」overwhelming military strength

> 表現のポイント ☞③
> people, countryなどの可算名詞とfewを組み合わせることで，数的な意味で，ほとんど〜ないという否定的意味を表すことができる。

5. 日米関係は長い歴史があるにもかかわらず，アメリカ人の中で日本の歴史，文化に精通している人は非常に少ない。
   ▶「精通している」be familiar with

> 表現のポイント 13④
> X is unlikely to do Y の形で，X が Y になる（をする）可能性は低い，という意味を表すことができる。

6. 現在の東アジア情勢から考えて，日米安保条約が近い将来破棄される可能性は極めて低い。
    ▶「日米安保条約」the US-Japan Security Treaty 「破棄する」abandon (or annul)

7. 日本人のアメリカ文化に対するあこがれが急速に衰える可能性は非常に低い。
    ▶「～に対するあこがれ」admiration for～ (or fascination with～)

― *LET'S TRY !* ―

A 'By the time S＋V, S＋V' の形で15 words以上の英文を書いてみましょう。

B 'be unlikely to V' の構文を使って10 words以上の英文を書いてみましょう。

UNIT 6
Drinking as part of youth culture

◆形容詞構文(1)

MODEL PASSAGE   *third-person essay*

以下の文章をCDで聴いてみましょう。また、①〜④の英文に注意しながら、繰り返し音読してみましょう。

　Just like their counterparts in other countries, Japanese college students love booze. They like the idea of getting drunk and having a good time. Freshmen in particular tend to drink too much, ①**partly because they are so happy to have all the pressures of entrance exams behind them.** ②**The really shocking thing is that almost every year some freshmen die of alcoholic poisoning**; typically, this happens at welcome parties right after the beginning of the new academic year in spring. One thing that is responsible for tragedies of this kind is a little game called *ikki-nomi*, in which someone gulps a glass of beer or other alcoholic beverage in one go, to the chanting of '*ikki, ikki, ikki*' by the others. Booze sometimes offers students, male or female, a one-way express ticket to heaven.

　Students seem to take every opportunity to drink: they drink at parties of all sorts, at club meetings, and at gatherings of their seminar groups, which often take place at *yakitori* shops, restaurants and bars. ③**"Drinking is relaxing, entertaining and lots of fun"**, they might say, but the problem is that they almost always drink too much, causing enormous inconvenience to people around them. Once they start drinking, many of them do not know when to stop. Intoxication often makes them sick, disorderly, or even violent. And drinking can ruin their health. ④**It is annoying and upsetting for a college teacher to find in his or her class a student suffering from a hangover as a result of excessive alcohol consumption the previous night.**

KEY CLAUSES

以下の日本語は，MODEL PASSAGEの重要構文①〜④の和訳です。本文を見ずに，この日本語から元の英文を作り上げる練習をしてみましょう。

① その理由の一つは入試のプレッシャーから解放されて彼らはとても明るい気分になっているためである。

② 大変衝撃的なことは，ほとんど毎年のように，新入生の中に急性アルコール中毒で死亡するものが出るということである。

③ 酒を飲むと気分がくつろぐし，それ自体が楽しいし，とってもおもしろい。

④ 大学の教師にとって，授業の時に，学生が前の晩の飲み過ぎがたたって二日酔い，という姿を見るのは不愉快であり，腹立たしくもある。

WORDS & PHRASES

次の日本語の意味に相当する英語を，MODEL PASSAGEの中から抜き出し，書き取ってみましょう。

1. 若者文化　　　　　　　＿＿＿＿＿＿＿＿＿＿＿＿＿＿
2. 酒　　　　　　　　　　＿＿＿＿＿＿＿＿＿＿＿＿＿＿
3. 一年生　　　　　　　　＿＿＿＿＿＿＿＿＿＿＿＿＿＿
4. 急性アルコール中毒　　＿＿＿＿＿＿＿＿＿＿＿＿＿＿
5. 悲劇　　　　　　　　　＿＿＿＿＿＿＿＿＿＿＿＿＿＿
6. がぶ飲みする　　　　　＿＿＿＿＿＿＿＿＿＿＿＿＿＿
7. 一気に（一息で）　　　＿＿＿＿＿＿＿＿＿＿＿＿＿＿
8. 迷惑　　　　　　　　　＿＿＿＿＿＿＿＿＿＿＿＿＿＿
9. 酩酊（酔っ払うこと）　＿＿＿＿＿＿＿＿＿＿＿＿＿＿
10. 二日酔い　　　　　　　＿＿＿＿＿＿＿＿＿＿＿＿＿＿

EXERCISES

次の日本語の文を英語に直しなさい。

> 表現のポイント ☞①
> 形容詞happyはbe happy to V, be happy that S+Vの形で「～してうれしい」，「～して満足している」などの意味を表す。ただし，will be happy to V, be happy that S+Vならば，「～（これから）するのはうれしい」，「喜んで～します」の意味になる点に注意。

1. Winston先生のオーラルイングリッシュでAをとれてとてもうれしい。一生けんめいにやるとやっただけのことはあるものだ。
   ▶「オーラルイングリッシュ」oral English 「一生けんめいにやるとやっただけのことはある」懸命の努力は報われる(rewarding)と考える。

2. 来週の土曜日のクラスコンパ，喜んで出席します。みんな楽しく過ごせるといいですね。
   ▶「クラスコンパ」class party

> 表現のポイント ☞②，③，④
> shocking, relaxing, entertaining, annoying, upsettingなどの形容詞は，ing形で表された感情を引き起こす対象が，主語となる点に注意。

3. 衝撃的なのは，飲み過ぎで肝炎にかかる学生がけっこういるという点だ。酒の飲み方がわかっていない学生が多いのは問題だ。
   ▶「肝炎」hepatitis 「酒の飲み方」酒の適切な飲み方(how to drink sensibly)と考える

4. ひなびた温泉の露天風呂に体を浸すのは実にゆったりした気分になるものだ。
   ▶「ひなびた（辺鄙なところにある）」remote countryside 「露天風呂」open-air bath

5. 酒を飲みながら，気の合う仲間同志でカラオケを歌うのはとても楽しいものだ。いいストレス発散になる。
   ▶「カラオケで歌う」sing *karaoke* 「ストレスを発散する」get rid of stress

6. 電車の中で酔っ払いが乗客にからんでいるいるのを見るのは実に不愉快だ。
   ▶ 「からむ」pester, pick a quarrel with 「不愉快」annoyingかupsettingを使う。

7. 現職の警察官が酔払い運転でつかまったと聞いて腹が立った。まったくあってはならないことだ。
   ▶ 「酔払い運転」drunken driving

― **LET'S TRY !**
| A | 'be happy to V' の構文を使って10 words以上の英文を書いてみましょう。

| B | 'What I think of drinking' というタイトルで100 words程度の英文を書いてみましょう。

I don't belong here

UNIT 7

◆形容詞構文(2)

MODEL PASSAGE   *first-person narrative*

以下の文章をCDで聴いてみましょう。また①〜④の英文に注意しながら，繰り返し音読してみましょう。

　Satoshi is 24 years old. He is working for a publisher in Tokyo. From the age of 10 to 17 he was in England with his family; his father was working there. A few years ago they came back to Japan. He graduated from a state university in Tokyo, and started to work at Yamato Publishing in Shibuya two years ago. His life back in Japan hasn't been too bad, but he has to admit he's still suffering from culture shock.

　To be honest, I'm still having trouble readjusting to Japanese culture. First, there are the language problems. ①**Before I went to England I'd never been irritated by the question of how to address other people and refer to myself in Japanese,** but now I sometimes wonder why Japanese has so many different ways of referring to 'I' and 'you'. ②**The other day, when I was at a party, I was a bit surprised to see one of my colleagues dexterously using a variety of first-person and second-person forms, depending on who he was talking to.** When he was chatting with a close friend, he was calling himself *ore*, and was referring to the friend as *omae*, but when he was with a mere acquaintance, he was using *boku* or *watashi* to refer to himself, and he called the person he was with *anata*, *kimi*, or *otaku*. And I remember him using *watakushi* to refer to himself when he was making a presentation at a business conference a couple of weeks ago. ③**Most foreigners studying Japanese must get confused over all the different forms of 'I' and 'you' in Japanese.** English has no variations on 'I' and 'you'. I sometimes find myself reluctant to speak Japanese because I have to choose the right first-person or second-person expressions for the situation.

In this country, being the same as other people seems to be less difficult than being different. For example, I like tea very much. When I was in England, I used to drink tea, with a lot of milk and sugar, a hundred times a day. And when I started working for this company, my old habit of having tea at breaks and at lunch time was still with me. But when I was drinking it, my superiors or colleagues often teased me: "Hey, you're constantly drinking tea with all that milk and sugar; you're really British, aren't you, Satoshi?" ④**I was a little shocked to realize my old habit made me noticeable in a funny way in the office.** That was just one of several things I've found uncomfortable back here in Japan. These days, to avoid standing out, I have green tea or soft drinks instead, just like everyone else in the office. I feel there's something strange in Japanese culture that makes people adopt uniform ways of doing things.

KEY CLAUSES

以下の日本語は，MODEL PASSAGEの重要構文①〜④の和訳です。本文を見ずに，この日本語から元の英文を作り上げる練習をしてみましょう。

① イギリスに行く前は，日本語で相手をなんと呼ぶか，また自分をどう呼ぶかという問題で頭を悩ませたことは一度もなかった。

② 先日宴会に出たとき，同僚のひとりが，自分がしゃべる相手によって，多種多様な一人称と二人称を実にうまく切り替えて使っていたのを見てすこし驚いてしまった。

③ 日本語を勉強しているほとんどの外国人はこういった日本語の「私」と「あなた」のいろいろな形には混乱してしまうに違いない。

④ 私の昔からの習慣のせいで自分が職場で変な具合に目立ってしまったことに気付いてちょっとショックだった。

WORDS & PHRASES

次の日本語の意味に相当する英語を，MODEL PASSAGEの中から抜き出し，書き取ってみましょう。

1. 出版社　　　　　＿＿＿＿＿＿＿＿＿＿＿＿＿＿＿＿
2. ことばの問題　　＿＿＿＿＿＿＿＿＿＿＿＿＿＿＿＿
3. 正直なところ（実を言えば）＿＿＿＿＿＿＿＿＿＿＿
4. 同僚　　　　　　＿＿＿＿＿＿＿＿＿＿＿＿＿＿＿＿
5. 知人　　　　　　＿＿＿＿＿＿＿＿＿＿＿＿＿＿＿＿
6. 一人称　　　　　＿＿＿＿＿＿＿＿＿＿＿＿＿＿＿＿
7. 二人称　　　　　＿＿＿＿＿＿＿＿＿＿＿＿＿＿＿＿
8. からかう　　　　＿＿＿＿＿＿＿＿＿＿＿＿＿＿＿＿
9. 清涼飲料　　　　＿＿＿＿＿＿＿＿＿＿＿＿＿＿＿＿
10. 画一的な　　　　＿＿＿＿＿＿＿＿＿＿＿＿＿＿＿＿

EXERCISES

次の日本語の文を英語に直しなさい。

> 表現のポイント　☞①，②，③，④
> irritated, surprised, confused, shockedなどの分詞形容詞は，文法的にはこれらの語句が表す感情の主体（人，機関，施設，生物など）が主語になる点に注意。X is shockedというとき，Xがショックを受けたという意味。

1. 日本語の敬語表現を正しく使うのがどれほど難しいかがわかってJohnは気分が落ちこんだ。
   ▶「敬語表現」honorific expressions　「気分が落ちこむ」be (get) depressed

2. イギリスでの生活にはとてもはやく慣れることができると聞いて由美は勇気づけられた。
   ▶「イギリスでの生活」the British way of life　「～に慣れる」adjust to～　「勇気づけられる」be (get) encouraged

3. Lucyは，日本語ではいろんな一人称，二人称の言いまわしがあると知って驚いた。
   ▶「言いまわし」forms

4. Henryは，友人の村越夫妻が自分の息子を紹介する時に「うちのバカ息子の晴男です」といったのには驚いた。
   ▶「村越夫妻」 Mr. and Mrs. Murakoshi

5. 義男は，英語の進行形が未来の意味を表す場合があると知って頭がわけがわからなくなった。
   ▶「進行形」progressive form

6. Kateは同じ漢字でも他の漢字との組み合わせ次第で全く読み方が変わる，ということを知って混乱してしまった。
   ▶「他の漢字との組み合わせ次第で」depending on what kanji it is combined with

7. 美由紀は新しい学校で自分が回りから疎外されているということを知ってショックだった。
   ▶「回りから疎外されている」回りが彼女を無視する，と考える。

8. 敏郎は信頼していた先生から「君は日本人なのに全然日本人らしくないね。みんなそう言ってるよ」といわれてものすごくショックだった。
   ▶「信頼する」trust

LET'S TRY!

A 'be (get) confused' の形を使って10 words以上の英文を書いてみましょう。

B 'be shocked' の形を使って15 words以上の英文を書いてみましょう。

UNIT 8
What's the purpose of work?

◆名詞構文

MODEL PASSAGE   *dialogue*

以下の文章をCDで聴いてみましょう。また、①〜④の英文に注意しながら、繰り返し音読してみましょう。

Kazuya works for a travel agency in Tokyo. He is 25 years old. It's two years since he started working there. At first he liked his job very much, but these days he finds himself rather unhappy with having to work so hard at the office. One day, Kazuya calls on his friend Frank. Frank works for the Tokyo office of British Airways. He has been there for three years. They are good friends. After lunch they talk over coffee; their talk focuses on the question 'What's the purpose of work?'

Kazuya: Frank, I sometimes wonder why I have to work so hard.

Frank: Isn't that what you want, Kazuya? You once told me how hard you work and how much you enjoy it.

Kazuya: Yes, I did. Perhaps that's because my father works so hard. He's been a *sake* brewer for more than 30 years. He's always telling me he does his job not just for money but also because it gives him spiritual satisfaction. He says ①**being a hard worker is a virtue in itself.**

Frank: So you're a kind of copy of your father. Like father, like son.

Kazuya: Well, I used to be, but these days I have my doubts about the value of hard work. It's not very pleasant to see my whole life revolving around work. In the office I have a huge amount of paperwork to do, and dealing with nagging customers is often time-consuming and exhausting. When I get home I'm too tired to do anything. What about you, Frank? Are you satisfied with your job?

Frank: Yes, I am. Like yours, my job is pretty tough; I have a lot of paperwork to do, and it's sometimes a strain to have to look at the PC display for so long. But I don't mind, because that's what I do for a living. I work for money and nothing else, and I'm happy that way. But Kazuya, don't get me wrong. ②**I'm not interested in money; I'm a pleasure seeker.** Spending money on holidays is really fantastic. ③**I feel I'm a real**

Kazuya: **traveler;** I've visited more than 20 countries so far. Hey, Kazuya, one thing I don't understand about what your father says is this 'spiritual satisfaction' that he says he gets from work. What does it mean?

Kazuya: He says he feels spiritual contentment when he's putting the whole of himself into work in an unselfish way, like a Buddhist monk achieving peace of mind through asceticism. His work is both mentally and physically rewarding, so he really enjoys working very hard. That's what he means.

Frank: Your father's a kind of philosopher, Kazuya, isn't he? He doesn't think of work just as something that gives him a financial return for his labor.

Kazuya: No, he doesn't. Japanese has a special expression, *kinro*, which is roughly equivalent to the English terms 'work' or 'labor' but has a different connotation. The word *kinro* implies a certain kind of positive and respectful attitude to work, which the terms 'work' or 'labor' don't. For my father, his work is his *kinro*.

Frank: I see. Well, Kazuya, your father may be a great teacher, or a great master of life, but you don't seem to have learned a lot from him. You sound unhappy with your job. Are you quitting?

Kazuya: Um, yes, I'm thinking of it. ④**But if I quit, people would say I was a loser, someone who gives up too easily.** I wouldn't like that.

Frank: Kazuya, if you feel your job is too much for you, there's no reason to stick to it. But if you learned to compartmentalize the pressures of hard work and found ways to relax, the way I have, you might find yourself happier with the work you're doing.

Kazuya: I know I can't afford to be choosy, but if I were offered a better job, I'd like to give it a try.

Frank: If that's your decision, go ahead, Kazuya. And good luck.

KEY CLAUSES

以下の日本語は，MODEL PASSAGEの重要構文①〜④の和訳です。本文を見ずに，この日本語から元の英文を作り上げる練習をしてみましょう。

① まじめに働くのはそれ自体美徳だよ。

② 僕はお金には興味はない。僕は人生を楽しむタイプの人間なんだ。

③ 僕は自分でも相当な旅行好きだと思ってるよ。

④ もし僕がやめたら，世間は僕のことをあいつは負け犬だ，すぐあきらめる奴だというだろうな。

WORDS & PHRASES

次の日本語の意味に相当する英語を，MODEL PASSAGEの中から抜き出し，書き取ってみましょう。

1. 旅行代理店　＿＿＿＿＿＿＿＿＿＿＿＿
2. 美徳　＿＿＿＿＿＿＿＿＿＿＿＿
3. 事務仕事　＿＿＿＿＿＿＿＿＿＿＿＿
4. 精神的満足　＿＿＿＿＿＿＿＿＿＿＿＿
5. 禁欲主義　＿＿＿＿＿＿＿＿＿＿＿＿
6. 哲学者　＿＿＿＿＿＿＿＿＿＿＿＿
7. 含みとしての意味　＿＿＿＿＿＿＿＿＿＿＿＿
8. （仏教の）僧侶　＿＿＿＿＿＿＿＿＿＿＿＿
9. 区分けする　＿＿＿＿＿＿＿＿＿＿＿＿
10. えり好みをする　＿＿＿＿＿＿＿＿＿＿＿＿

EXERCISES

次の日本語の文を英語に直しなさい。

> 表現のポイント
> 英語では〜をする人（もの）を表す接尾辞er，anなどを活用することで日本語ならば動詞的表現になるところを簡潔に名詞化して表すことができる。
>
> 例：「君は運転が上手だ」You're a good driver.
> 　　「Clarkは歌がとてもうまい」Clark is an excellent singer.
> 　　「Dianは音楽の天分がある」Dian is a gifted musician.

1. 仕事ぶりがまじめだということは必ずしも仕事ができるということではない。
   ▶「仕事ができる」be a competent worker

2. Judyは細かいことにうるさいタイプの人間だから，職場ではみんな距離をおいているよ。
   ▶「細かいことにうるさい」nitpicker

3. 今度新しく入ってきた武藤君はカッコよくて，なんかさわやかな感じなので，隠れファンがけっこういるんだ。
   ▶「カッコいい」cool 「隠れファン」secret admirer

4. Davidは勤勉で人柄もいい人間なんだが勤める先々でリストラにあい，だんだん酒に溺れるようになってしまった。今では全く人生の負け組だ。
   ▶「リストラにあう」be fired 「負け組み」loser

5. 生まれつきもめごとの調停をやっているようなのもいるかと思えば，生まれた時からもめごとを起こしているような感じの人間もいる。
   ▶「もめごとの調停者」peacemaker 「もめごとを起こす人」troublemaker

6. この会社へ就職を希望するんだったら，英語がよく話せることが必要な条件のひとつです。
   ▶「就職を希望する」就職希望者と考えればapplicantが使える。

7. 肉体労働に従事している人がデスクワークをやっている人たちよりも人間として劣るなどと考えるのは大変な間違いである。
   ▶「肉体労働に従事している人」blue-collar worker 「デスクワークをやっている人たち」white-collar workerなどが使える。

LET'S TRY !

A MODEL PASSAGEにあるような '形容詞 + er (or an, st, etc.) 型の名詞' を使って10 words以上の英文を書いてみましょう。

B 'What do people get from work?' というタイトルで100 words程度の英文を書いてみましょう。

The Japanese as half-Asian

UNIT 9

◆時制── 過去と過去完了

MODEL PASSAGE　*third-person essay*

以下の文章をCDで聴いてみましょう。また①〜④の英文に注意しながら、繰り返し音読してみましょう。

　Japan is an Asian country, and this is true in terms of race, culture, and geography. But one soon notices that Japanese history includes something alien to the histories of other Asian nations. An overview of modern Asian history shows that Japan alone was an imperialist country, colonizing Korea, Taiwan and Manchuria for exploitation. Imperialism in modern times was exemplified by Great Powers in the West such as Britain, Germany, France, Russia, and America. ①**By the time Japan emerged as a modern nation, about three-quarters of the earth had been colonized and was under the control of Western empires.** ②**Japan fanatically followed their example, desperate to be recognized as a new member of the Great-Power club.** ③**History shows that the Japanese Empire ruined itself because of the un-Asian action it took.**

　Today, many Japanese people realize how wrong they were in the past. What many Japanese regret most is that this imperialistic behavior during the first half of the twentieth century gave neighboring nations such a bad impression of this small island state. Their attitude changed somewhat after the end of the Pacific War, ④**but before that their image of Japan had been that of an aggressive, warlike country.** This fixed image has not entirely gone even today, when Japan is no longer a military power. It is not surprising that what Japan did in the past makes Chinese or Koreans feel the Japanese are somewhat alien, but the majority of Japanese people do wish other Asian people to understand that imperialist Japan was an isolated exception in the very long history of the country, and that the Japanese are essentially a peace-loving people, sincerely hoping to get along with the rest of the world.

KEY CLAUSES

以下の日本語は，MODEL PASSAGEの重要構文①〜④の和訳です。本文を見ずに，この日本語から元の英文を作り上げる練習をしてみましょう。

① 日本が近代国家として台頭した頃には，地球のおよそ4分の3は西洋の帝国主義国家群によって植民地化され，その支配下にあった。

② 日本はそれらの国家に追随することに狂奔し，列強クラブの新規加入会員として認知してもらおうと懸命だった。

③ 歴史が示すところでは，日本帝国は非アジア的な振る舞いをしたことで，自滅の道をたどったのである。

④ しかしそれ以前は，近隣諸国の日本に対するイメージは，攻撃的で，戦争好きの国家である，というものだった。

WORDS & PHRASES

次の日本語の意味に相当する英語を，MODEL PASSAGEの中から抜き出し，書き取ってみましょう。

1. 地理 _____
2. 異質な _____
3. 帝国主義国家 _____
4. 植民地化する _____
5. 搾取 _____
6. 例証する _____
7. 台頭する _____
8. 日本帝国 _____
9. 好戦的な _____
10. 軍事大国 _____

EXERCISES

次の日本語の文を英語に直しなさい。

> 表現のポイント ☞ ①, ④
> 一般に過去完了は，過去の事柄（もしくは過去形で表現された事柄）に時の参照点（または基準点）がおかれている場合に，その過去の事柄との関連で，それより古い時制として使うのが基本的用法。例：I had been teaching math for five years before I realized that teaching was not in my blood.（自分が教師に向いていないということがわかる前に私は数学の教師を5年間していた。＝私は5年間数学の教師をやってみてやっと自分が教師に向いていないことがわかった。）

1. 第一次世界大戦が終わる頃には日本は世界の列強の一員として認められるようになっていた。
   ▶「第一次世界大戦」World War Ⅰ　「認める」recognize

2. 1930年代の終わりには日本は国際的な孤立を深めていた。これが後の国家的悲劇へとつながっていったのである。
   ▶「終わりには」byで表す。　「国際的な」世界中から from the rest of the worldと考える　「孤立する」isolate　「悲劇」tragedy

3. 英米との戦争に突入する前に日本は中国と数年にわたって交戦していた。
   ▶「戦争に突入する」go to war against (or with)～　「交戦している」be fighting against

4. 1940年頃には日米関係は危機的な状況を迎えていた。
   ▶「頃には」byで表す。　「日米関係」The US-Japan relationship

> 表現のポイント ☞ ②, ③
> いわゆる物語形式で，過去の事柄が，継起的に event 1, event 2, and event 3 という風に並列的に述べられる場合，すべてを過去形で表現し，①の場合のような，時の参照点と，それを基準にした過去完了という時制の落差を表す必要はない。②と③をそれぞれ event 1, event 2 とすると，両者ともに過去時制が適切であり，event 1 の方が event 2 よりも古いと考えて過去完了にする必要はない。

5. 日露戦争に勝利してのち，日本は帝国主義的様相を一段と深めていった。そしてそのことが欧米列強を刺激する結果になったのである。
    ▶「日露戦争」The Russo-Japanese War 「帝国主義的」imperialistic 「〜を刺激する結果になる」end up offending〜

6. 1945年8月に第2次世界大戦が終わり，その後日本は連合国側に占領された。この戦争で日本は植民地の全てを失い，およそ300万人の犠牲者をだした。
    ▶「第2次世界大戦」 World War II 「連合国側」Allied Forces

7. 戦後日本は戦争を放棄し，経済大国への道を邁進したが，これは日本人の価値観の大転換を意味した。
    ▶「放棄する」renounce 「経済大国」economic power 「邁進する」try hard 「価値観」values

― *LET'S TRY !* ―

A 'by the time S + V(過去)，S + V(過去完了)' の組み合わせで15 words以上の英文を書いてみましょう。

B 本文の②と③の組み合わせを参考にして，過去形の文を継起的に使って20 words以上の英文を書いてみましょう。

Why few Japanese can speak English

UNIT 10

◆接続詞

MODEL PASSAGE　*third-person essay*

以下の文章をCDで聴いてみましょう。また，①〜⑤の英文に注意しながら，繰り返し音読してみましょう。

　It's well known that most Japanese cannot speak English even after studying it for six years at junior and senior high school. Why is this? ① **Perhaps the biggest reason is that they have little motivation to learn to speak English.** When Japanese students say they are good at English, it usually means they are test-wise, capable of getting high scores in English exams, and it certainly doesn't mean that they are fluent speakers of English. In Japan, the main purpose of English classes in secondary schools is to prepare the students for high-school and college entrance exams. And those entrance exams don't include any direct test of the examinees' speaking ability. ② **Moreover, the exams are set in such a way that they favor students trained in the traditional grammar-translation method.** In short, students are not encouraged to speak English. ③**That is why their command of English is generally poor.**

　There is another important reason why most Japanese are poor speakers of English. As a rule, one learns something best when one has to learn it in order to survive. This is never more true than with language study. If Japanese students were put in a situation in which speaking English was a must for them to survive, ④**they'd no doubt learn to speak it, no matter how difficult they found it.** Japan, as an advanced country, is both fortunate and unfortunate not to be in that situation. For many Japanese, the ability to speak English is nothing more than a brand-name accessory like a Gucci handbag or a Chanel suit. Those items are normally bought for show, not for survival. ⑤**This helps to account for the fact that only a few Japanese can speak good English.**

KEY CLAUSES

以下の日本語は，MODEL PASSAGEの重要構文①〜⑤の和訳です。本文を見ずに，この日本語から元の英文を作り上げる練習をしてみましょう。

① 恐らく最も大きな理由は，彼等には英会話を学習する動機がほとんどないということであろう。

② それに加えて，試験問題は伝統的な文法・訳読中心の学習法で鍛えられてきた学生に有利なように作られている。

③ そういうわけで彼等の英語運用能力は一般的に低いのである。

④ それがどれほど難しくても，彼らは間違いなく英語を話せるようになるであろう。

⑤ このことが，英語が上手に話せる日本人が少ないことの説明として役立つだろう。

WORDS & PHRASES

次の日本語の意味に相当する英語を，MODEL PASSAGEの中から抜き出し，書き取ってみましょう。

1. 動機　　　　　　　　＿＿＿＿＿＿＿＿＿＿＿＿＿＿＿
2. テストに強い　　　　＿＿＿＿＿＿＿＿＿＿＿＿＿＿＿
3. 会話能力　　　　　　＿＿＿＿＿＿＿＿＿＿＿＿＿＿＿
4. 〜に有利に働く　　　＿＿＿＿＿＿＿＿＿＿＿＿＿＿＿
5. 受験生　　　　　　　＿＿＿＿＿＿＿＿＿＿＿＿＿＿＿
6. 文法・訳読的方法　　＿＿＿＿＿＿＿＿＿＿＿＿＿＿＿
7. 英語の運用能力　　　＿＿＿＿＿＿＿＿＿＿＿＿＿＿＿
8. やらなければならないこと　＿＿＿＿＿＿＿＿＿＿＿＿＿
9. ブランドの　　　　　＿＿＿＿＿＿＿＿＿＿＿＿＿＿＿
10. 説明する　　　　　　＿＿＿＿＿＿＿＿＿＿＿＿＿＿＿

EXERCISES

次の日本語の文を英語に直しなさい。

> 表現のポイント ☞①
> センテンスの中で，接続詞thatが導く名詞節が補語節として使われることがある。

1. 日本の中高生が英語を勉強する最大の理由は英語が入試で出されるからです。
   ▶「入試」entrance exams

2. 日本の英語教育の大きな問題の一つは，学生が実際に英語を話す機会が少ないという点です。
   ▶「日本の英語教育」English education in Japan

> 表現のポイント ☞②
> 様態を表す構文として，「that以下の状態になるように」という意味で，in such a way that S＋Vの形を用いることができる。

3. この和英辞書は英語の初心者でも基本的運用力がつくように編集されています。
   ▶「基本的運用力」basic command 「つく」develop 「編集されている」be edited

> 表現のポイント ☞③
> 「そういうわけで（だから）～なのだ」はThis (that) is why S＋Vであらわすことができる。この場合，this (that) は前文の内容を受け，それを原因ととらえ，why以下がその結果である，ということを表す。This (that) is whyは形式ばった表現ではThereforeにあたる。

4. 今うちの学生は大学入試のことで頭が一杯です。そういうわけで彼らは実用英語に関心を示さないのです。
   ▶「実用英語」practical English

5. うちの姉は来年からアメリカの大学に２年間留学することになっています。そういうわけで，姉は今必死で英会話の勉強に励んでいるというわけです。
   ▶「英会話」spoken English

> 表現のポイント ☞ ④
> no matter how (however) + 副詞(形容詞) + S + Vの形で,「どんなに～しても」という譲歩の意味を表すことができる。

6. どんなに一生懸命にいいきかせても,うちの弟は単語を覚えるのが面倒くさい,といって英語の勉強をやろうとはしません。
   ▶「面倒くさい」troublesome, bothersome

7. どんなにがんばったって,加藤先生の英語学はAをとれそうもないよ。
   ▶「英語学」English linguistics

> 表現のポイント ☞ ⑤
> 名詞のfactは同格節としてthat節をしたがえることができる。

8. 年間2000万人近い日本人が海外に出かけているという事実は,海外旅行が日本人にとって全くありふれたものになってしまったということを表している。
   ▶「ありふれた」common

LET'S TRY!

A 'S + V, and that is why S + V' を使って15 words以上の英文を書いてみましょう。

B 'English as a means of cross-cultural communication' というタイトルで100 words程度の英文を書いてみましょう。

48

UNIT 11
How I wish I could live on my own!

◆助動詞

MODEL PASSAGE   *first-person narrative*

以下の文章をCDで聴いてみましょう。また①〜⑦の英文に注意しながら、繰り返し音読してみましょう。

Yumi, who's 19, is studying law at a university in Fukuoka. She has no brothers or sisters. Her father works for a car manufacturer, and her mother is a math teacher at junior high school. Twice a week Yumi teaches at a small juku near the university. She gets on well with her father but not so well with her mother, who is always fussing over her. She would like to leave home and live by herself somewhere.

This morning Mother told me, yet again, "①**Yumi, you'd better start thinking about working for the government when you graduate from university.** If you're a government employee, you're very unlikely to lose your job, ②**and you'll be free from money worries for the rest of your life.** Look, I'm saying this for your own good!" Mother says this so often that it's ringing in my ears. She isn't a bad person; I know how much she loves me, but she often gets fussy and bossy, and starts telling me what to do. I'm the only child in my family, ③**and I sometimes feel this may be a disadvantage,** because I get too much love and attention from my parents. Mother's been keeping a watchful eye on me ever since I was born; ④**she's the kind of woman who does everything she can to keep her daughter away from the slightest hint of risk or danger.** She's always suggesting that I should choose what's safe and stable. I've ended up feeling I'm a kind of prisoner; ⑤**a psychologist would call me a victim of 'smothering love'.**

Father is much more reasonable and understanding. He often says, "Yumi, ⑥**you have to do your best to live your own life.** I work for a car company, and I'm very happy with my job because it's what I've always wanted to do." My dream is to be a lawyer. I know passing the bar exam will be quite a challenge, but I'm determined to try, because I don't want my life to be just 'safe and stable'.

Recently I've been getting fed up with having to commute every day. It takes about two hours to get from home to the university—it's a long and tiring journey. And when I teach at the *juku* I don't get home until around midnight. I'd like to live on my own, away from home. But to do that, I need money. I was thinking of quitting my job at the *juku* next year, ⑦**but I might as well do it for a bit longer**—perhaps until I've made enough money to pay the deposit if I rent a flat. Oh, it's time I started cooking something for dinner. Father and Mother are both at work today, so it's my turn—I almost forgot!

KEY CLAUSES

以下の日本語は，MODEL PASSAGEの重要構文①〜⑦の和訳です。本文を見ずに，この日本語から元の英文を作り上げる練習をしてみましょう。

① 由美，大学を卒業したら公務員になる，という風に考え始めたほうがいいんじゃないの。

② そしたら一生お金の苦労はしなくて済むよ。

③ そして，時々思うんだけれど，一人っ子というのは両親の愛情と関心が強すぎて，かえってよくないんじゃないかしら。

④ うちの母は，自分の娘がどんな小さな危険にもあわないようにするために全力を尽くすというタイプの女性です。

⑤ 心理学者は私のことを'愛情過多の犠牲者'と呼ぶでしょう。

⑥ おまえは自分の人生を生きるために最善を尽くさなければいけないよ。

⑦ でも，もう少し長く続けるのも悪くはないかもね。

WORDS & PHRASES

次の日本語の意味に相当する英語を，MODEL PASSAGEの中から抜き出し，書き取ってみましょう。

1. 公務員 _____
2. 口やかましい _____
3. いばり散らす _____
4. 不利益 _____
5. 囚人 _____
6. 心理学者 _____
7. うっとうしいほどの愛情 _____
8. 司法試験 _____
9. （難しくて）やりがいのあること _____
10. 敷金 _____

EXERCISES

次の日本語の文を英語に直しなさい。

> 表現のポイント ☞①
> had betterは「〜しないと不利益になる，ためにならない」などのニュアンスを含むadviceをあたえる場合に使われる。その意味合いがあるために，使い方によっては相手に対する恫喝，脅しの意味が出る場合がある。会話ではhad betterよりも，'d betterの形が普通である点に注意。

1. 店長の言うとおりにしておいた方がいいよ。さもないとクビになるかもしれないからね。
   ▶「店長」manager

> **表現のポイント** ☞②
> willにはさまざまのはたらきがあるが，そのうち一般的なもののひとつとして'未来に関する推量'がある。

2. 父の会社はかなり経営状態が悪いらしい。2，3年以内につぶれるといううわさだ。
   ▶「～といううわさだ」there is a rumor (rumor has it) that～

> **表現のポイント** ☞③
> mayの最も一般的なはたらきとして'推量の表現，可能性への言及'があげられる。

3. 兄弟がいるのもあまりよくないかもしれない。なぜかというと，兄弟というのは性格が全く異なることが多く，そのためあらそいが起こりやすいためである。
   ▶「性格」personality (temperament) 「あらそい」arguments (disputes)

> **表現のポイント** ☞④
> canの最も一般的なはたらきの一つは「～できる」という意味，すなわち'能力への言及'である。

4. 私の同僚のJackは昇進のためだったらできることは何でもするというタイプの男だ。
   ▶「同僚」colleague 「昇進する」gain (or win) promotion

> **表現のポイント** ☞⑤
> wouldの用法の一つとして，「～ならば～であろう」の「～であろう」の部分にあたるような'仮定条件の帰結'を表すはたらきが挙げられる。

5. まともなホストファミリーならホームステイしている学生を置き去りにして旅行に出かけたりはしないでしょう。
   ▶「まともな」respectable

> **表現のポイント** ☞⑥
> have toはほぼmustとほぼ同じ意味で用いられるが，特に口語ではhave toのほうがmustより好まれる傾向がある。その理由のひとつはmustに比べてhave toのほうが口調が柔らかく感じられるため。

6. あなたはただ会社でまじめに働いてお金を持ってきてくれればいいのよ。
   ▶All you have to do is〜の構文が使える。

> 表現のポイント　☞⑦
> might as wellは，2つの選択肢（どちらも比較的内容の軽い事柄）のうちどちらをとってもたいした違いはないが，あえて言えば，一方をとっても悪くはない，というような消極的選択を表す。なおmay as wellもmight as wellと同じように使うことが可能。

7. どこかに何か食べに行くのもいいが，すしの出前を取るのも悪くないね。
   ▶「すしの出前を取る」order some sushi from〜

8. 「夏休みどうするつもり？」「北海道の友達のところに1週間ほど泊りに行こうかなあなんて思っているけれど，カナダかオーストラリアを2，3週間の一人旅なんてのも悪くないかもね。」
   ▶「2，3週間の一人旅」go to〜for a couple of weeks by oneself

LET'S TRY !

A　'had better' を使って10 words以上の英文を書いてみましょう。

B　'might as well' を使って10 words以上の英文を書いてみましょう。

UNIT 11

UNIT 12
The pros and cons of so-called 'exam English'

◆感覚・認識動詞

MODEL PASSAGE   *dialogue*

以下の文章をCDで聴いてみましょう。また①〜⑤の英文に注意しながら、繰り返し音読してみましょう。

   John is a 28-year-old Englishman. He has been in Japan for five years, teaching English at a language school in Shinjuku. Takeshi, aged 29, is an English teacher at a high school in Tokyo. They are good friends. John is visiting Takeshi at his flat; they are discussing 'exam English' in Japan.

John: Hey, Takeshi, a couple of days ago one of my students, a high school boy, came up to me and asked me to solve English problems in an exam set by a certain state university in Japan.

Takeshi: So you gave it a try?

John: Yes, I did.

Takeshi: How did you get on?

John: Well, as a matter of fact I couldn't do even half of them. If I'd taken the exam, I'd certainly have failed, ha! ha! No, it's no laughing matter. ① **One thing I noticed was how much Japanese they used in the exam.** The instructions were all in Japanese, so I understood barely half of them. Besides, quite a large part of the exam was translation from English into Japanese. ②**This made me think the examiners weren't particularly interested in finding out how well the examinees could use English.** Their main interest was in seeing how well they knew Japanese.

Takeshi: Oh, come on, John. That's going too far. Look, exams of that kind are primarily for Japanese students wanting to get into Japanese colleges. That's why so much Japanese is used or required.

John: Well, it seems odd to me, Takeshi. OK, let's imagine the opposite situation. If you were sitting for a Japanese test, and you saw lots of English used in it, would you feel like calling it a Japanese test?

Takeshi: I see what you mean. ③**But I think the people who make exam questions like the ones you tried know what they're doing.**

John: What do you mean, Takeshi?

Takeshi: Well, a lot of Japanese teachers of English have a traditional idea that if you can put certain English structures into proper Japanese, that shows that you're smart. Actually, there are certain types of structures that they use for translation problems over and over again.

John: ④**That sounds interesting!** What sort of structures do you have in mind? Give me one or two examples.

Takeshi: Sentences including ellipsis, or inversion, for example. Let me think… OK, take this one, 'This process consists of part A and part B, and that process part C and part D.' If you understand that the verb phrase 'consists of' is omitted in the second clause, then you'll be considered intelligent.

John: So you mean English exam problems in Japan are a kind of intelligence test? They aren't necessarily testing your command of English?

Takeshi: ⑤**John, you sound a bit too extreme again!** Examinees usually have to answer a lot of problems in a short time, and those problems often include writing English passages of certain length. And listening comprehension tests are very common these days. I believe what's called 'exam English' in Japan is generally useful in testing whether examinees have the working knowledge of English they're supposed to have.

John: I'm not sure about that. The student who asked me about the exam can't speak English very well. He says he always gets an A grade in English tests at school, but he says all the English words and phrases and sentence structures he learns are ones that are likely to come up in exams. He isn't interested in whether he'll actually be able to use them.

Takeshi: Mm… That's the problem. I wonder if it would be possible to give speaking tests as part of college entrance exams. If so, the exams would be a lot more meaningful.

KEY CLAUSES

以下の日本語は，MODEL PASSAGEの重要構文①〜⑤の和訳です。本文を見ずに，この日本語から元の英文を作り上げる練習をしてみましょう。

① 一つ気付いたのは，その試験にはたくさんの日本語が使われていたという点だ。

② このことで私が思ったのは，試験官は受験生がどの程度英語の運用能力があるかを知ることに特に関心があるわけじゃない，ということだ。

③ しかし私は，君が解いてみたような試験問題を作る人たちは，自分達が何をしているのかということについてはよくわきまえている，と思うよ。

④ それはおもしろい（おもしろく聞こえる）。

⑤ ジョン，それはまたちょっと言い過ぎだよ。

WORDS & PHRASES

次の日本語の意味に相当する英語を，MODEL PASSAGEの中から抜き出し，書き取ってみましょう。

1. 語学学校　　　　　　　　＿＿＿＿＿＿＿＿＿＿＿＿＿＿＿＿
2. 受験英語　　　　　　　　＿＿＿＿＿＿＿＿＿＿＿＿＿＿＿＿
3. （問題の）指示文　　　　＿＿＿＿＿＿＿＿＿＿＿＿＿＿＿＿
4. 試験官　　　　　　　　　＿＿＿＿＿＿＿＿＿＿＿＿＿＿＿＿
5. 受験生　　　　　　　　　＿＿＿＿＿＿＿＿＿＿＿＿＿＿＿＿
6. 試験問題　　　　　　　　＿＿＿＿＿＿＿＿＿＿＿＿＿＿＿＿
7. 省略　　　　　　　　　　＿＿＿＿＿＿＿＿＿＿＿＿＿＿＿＿
8. 倒置　　　　　　　　　　＿＿＿＿＿＿＿＿＿＿＿＿＿＿＿＿
9. 知能テスト　　　　　　　＿＿＿＿＿＿＿＿＿＿＿＿＿＿＿＿
10. リスニングテスト　　　　＿＿＿＿＿＿＿＿＿＿＿＿＿＿＿＿

EXERCISES

次の日本語の文を英語に直しなさい。

> 表現のポイント ☞①
> noticeは主として目で見たり，その他の感覚器官で認識できる事柄に気付く，という意味で使われることが多い。この点で，気付く対象が主として，思考的内容の場合に用いられるrealizeとは用法が異なることに注意
> 例：I realized how selfish I had been（私はいかに自分が身勝手であったかがわかった。）

1. 私は英語の試験問題の中に文法上の誤りがあることに気付いた。試験問題はもっと慎重に作成してもらいたいものだ。
   ▶「文法上の誤り」grammatical mistake 「作成する」set

2. 自分の英語力が以前より落ちていることに気付いた。半年怠けると英語の語彙力ががた落ちになった感じがする。
   ▶ここでの「気付く」はnoticeか realizeか？ 「英語力が落ちている」be worse at English than〜の形で表せる。「語彙力」vocabulary

> 表現のポイント ☞②
> find outは調査，努力の結果，ある情報，ことがらを見つけるという意味で使われる。
> この点で，「見つける」「〜ということが（経験的に）わかる」という意味で用いられるfindとは用法が異なることに注意。
> 例：I found the missing bag in the room（見あたらなかったバッグがその部屋でみつかった。） I found the movie boring（その映画は退屈だった。）

3. どうして日本の学生は英語をコミュニケーションの手段としてとらえていないのかについて調べてみたい。
   ▶「AをBととらえる」see A as B, think of A as B 「調べる」はfindかfind outか？

4. 私にとっては，英文和訳は退屈でうっとうしい。英文和訳をしていると日本語をどう組み立てるかばかりに気をとられるのがいやなんです。
   ▶個人的主観の表現はfindか find outか？ 「英文和訳」putting English into Japanese 「うっとうしい」bothersome 「組み立てる」construct

> **表現のポイント** ☞③
> knowは「知る」,「わかる」といった動作動詞ではなく「知っている」,「わかっている」という意味の状態動詞である点に注意。この点で,「知る」,「認識する」という意味で使われるtellとは用法が異なることに注意。
> 例：Can you tell genuine diamonds from false ones?「本物のダイヤとにせのダイヤの区分けができますか。」

5. 日本の学生は，高校卒業までにどのくらいの英単語を学習することになっているかあなたは知っていますか。
    ▶「高校卒業」finish high school 　「学習することになっているか」be supposed to learn

6. Johnのなまりで，彼がスコットランド出身ということがわかるよ。スコットランドの英語とイングランドの英語はかなり違うからね。
    ▶「なまり」accent　「スコットランド」Scotland　ここでの「わかる」はknowかtellか？

> **表現のポイント** ☞④,⑤
> soundはあとに形容詞相当語句を従えて，「～のように聞こえる」（相手の発話の印象）という意味を表す。この点で，look＋形容詞相当語句が表す，「～のように見える」（相手の見かけ，容姿，外見の印象）という意味とは用法が異なることに注意。例：You look tired.（あなたは疲れているみたいだ。）

7. ずい分怒っていらっしゃるようなお話しぶりですね。気持ちを落ち着かせてもっと理性的にものを考えられたらいかがですか。
    ▶「もっと理性的に」more rationally

8. 英文学のMilton教授は実際の年齢よりもずいぶん老けてみえます。きっとご苦労が多かったのでしょう。
    ▶「英文学」English literature　ここでの「みえる」はsoundかlookか？

LET'S TRY !

A 動詞 'notice' をつかって10 words以上の英文を書いてみましょう。

B 'Why I'm learning English' というタイトルで100 words程度の英文を書いてみましょう。

An aging society

UNIT **13**

◆比較級(1)

MODEL PASSAGE *third-person essay*

以下の文章をCDで聞いてみましょう。また，①〜④の英文に注意しながら，繰り返し音読してみましょう。

　Japan, even more than other developed countries, faces the pressures of an aging population. ①**The proportion of people in their seventies is now about three times what it was fifty years ago**, and is expected to rise a great deal higher.

　There are two main reasons for this. The first is that the birth rate has been falling for more than twenty years. ②**More and more women are going out to work**; now there are about a third as many women in full-time employment as men. ③**This means that fewer women choose to have children**, and those who do are having them later; ④**the later a woman has children, the fewer she is likely to have.**

　The other reason, which is far more important, is that people are living longer than ever before. Diet, sanitation and living conditions have all improved remarkably in the last couple of decades, and there have been amazing advances in medicine.

What problems does an aging population bring? There are more frail or disabled people, but fewer younger people to take care of them. There is an increasing burden on health services. There is pressure on state and company pensions, which have to be paid to more elderly people and for many more years. All these problems will combine to make the Japanese economy less and less productive.

KEY CLAUSES

以下の日本語は，MODEL PASSAGEの重要構文①〜④の和訳です。本文を見ずに，この日本語から元の英文を作り上げる練習をしてみましょう。

① 70歳代の人の割合は50年前に比べて3倍になっている。

② 社会に出て働く女性の数がどんどん増えてきている。

③ このことは，子供を持とうと考える女性の数がどんどん減ってきているということである。

④ 出産年齢が上がれば上がるほど，生む子供の数が減ってくる。

WORDS & PHRASES

次の日本語の意味に相当する英語を，MODEL PASSAGEの中から抜き出し，書き取ってみましょう。

1. 直面する　　　　　　　　_____
2. 人口の老齢化　　　　　　_____
3. 出生率　　　　　　　　　_____
4. 正社員雇用　　　　　　　_____
5. 衛生　　　　　　　　　　_____
6. 生活状態　　　　　　　　_____
7. 虚弱な　　　　　　　　　_____
8. 身体障害者　　　　　　　_____
9. 保健（厚生）サービス　　_____
10. 年金　　　　　　　　　　_____

EXERCISES

次の日本語の文を英語に直しなさい。

> **表現のポイント** ☞①
> 倍数詞を使う比較表現においては，倍数詞を含む部分が文全体の補語か副詞の働きをする場合，three times as strong as〜, twice as fast as〜などのように，as〜asの中身が一語だけになる。それに対して倍数詞を含む部分が文全体の中で動詞の目的語か，there is構文のbe動詞以下の部分にあたる場合，three times as many books as〜, などのようにas〜asのなかに名詞が入りこむ点に注意。ただし①の場合のように，倍数詞表現の直後にwhatを使った構文がくることもある。

1. この国の医療費は20年前に比べると2倍に増えている。
   ▶「医療費」medical expenses

2. 日本における100歳以上のお年寄りの数はこの40年でおよそ150倍に達している。
   ▶「100歳以上のお年寄り」centenarian

> **表現のポイント** ☞②
> 日本語の「〜が増加している（増加した）」は英語ではmore and more＋名詞表現を文の主語として設定すると，簡潔な構文ができあがる。

3. 老人介護などの福祉関係の仕事に携わる人の数がどんどん増えてきている。
   ▶「老人介護」nursing the elderly 「福祉関係の仕事」welfare work

4 世界で最も急速に高齢化が進んでいる日本では，老後の生活が心配だと考える人の数が増えてきている。
   ▶「高齢化」aging 「老後の生活」老後をどう生きるか 'how they will manage in their old age' と考える。

> **表現のポイント** ☞③
> ②とは逆に，日本語の「〜が減少している（減少した）」は英語ではfewer and fewer＋名詞表現を文の主語として設定すると，簡潔な構文ができあがる。ただし，この場合の名詞表現が非加算名詞の場合fewer and fewerではなく，less and lessになる点に注意。

UNIT 13

5. 女性の価値観が変わってきたせいか，結婚して家庭を築きたいと考える女性の数が減ってきている。
   ▶「価値観」values

6. このまま不況が続けば，定年退職後に豊かな生活を送ることのできる人はいよいよ少なくなるであろう。
   ▶「不況」recession 「定年退職後」after retirement 「豊かな生活」comfortable life

表現のポイント ☞ ④
the＋比較級＋主語＋動詞句の形で「〜すればするほど〜する」という比例関係的意味を表すことができる。

7. お年寄りの数が多ければ多いほど国家の生産性はおちる，と一般に考えられている。
   ▶「生産性」productivity

8. 出生率が下がれば下がるほど，教育関連産業はより大きな打撃を受けるであろう。
   ▶「出生率」birth rate 「教育関連産業」education-related industries

LET'S TRY!

A ①のような，倍数詞を使った比較構文を使って10 words以上の英文を書いてみましょう。

B ④にならって，'the＋比較級＋S＋V，the＋比較級＋S＋V' の構文を使って15 words以上の英文を書いてみましょう。

UNIT 14
Do we have to live in a polluted environment?

◆比較級(2)

MODEL PASSAGE   *third-person essay*

以下の文章をCDで聴いてみましょう。また①~②の英文に注意しながら，繰り返し音読してみましょう。

The miraculous development of science and technology since the Industrial Revolution has opened Pandora's box. The remarkable strides mankind has made have yielded a great variety of modern comforts, but the cost has been high, perhaps too high. The most keenly-felt loss is that of a clean environment. ①**Never before has the earth been as badly polluted as it is today.** Rivers and lakes are being contaminated by harmful chemicals from factories and homes. The oceans are being polluted by the dumping of poisonous substances. The exhaust fumes cars emit are contributing to a drastic increase in the amount of carbon dioxide in the air. In the last couple of decades, people have been warned of the great dangers posed by chemicals like dioxins, CFCs, and environmental hormones, all of which are now threatening the very survival of the human race.

Being eco-friendly is a new principle that many people have begun to adopt, and there is hope that corporations and countries will follow; but ②**nothing could be a greater challenge than trying to return the environment to the pollution-free state it must have been in before the Industrial Revolution.** The reason is clear. To do that, people would have to adopt a much simpler lifestyle, without cars, planes, air conditioners, detergent, and so on. For most people today, doing without these things would be unthinkable.

We humans have always tried to make life safer, easier and more comfortable, but until recently we hadn't realized that the price we would have to pay would be a more polluted world. Now that the true scale of the problem is coming home to us, we are faced with difficult decisions. If we really want to stop things getting worse, we have to be ready to put up with a much less comfortable life. But how many people would, for example, be willing to use their cars less often, or even do without them at all? Some environmentalists fear that we will not take action until it is too late.

KEY CLAUSES

以下の日本語は，MODEL PASSAGEの重要構文①～②の和訳です。本文を見ずに，この日本語から元の英文を作り上げる練習をしてみましょう。

① 今日ほど地球が汚染された時代はかつてなかった。

② 産業革命以前の汚染されていない環境を回復しようとすることほど困難なことはないであろう。

WORDS & PHRASES

次の日本語の意味に相当する英語を，MODEL PASSAGEの中から抜き出し，書き取ってみましょう。

1. 奇跡的な　　　　　　＿＿＿＿＿＿＿＿＿＿＿＿＿
2. 産業革命　　　　　　＿＿＿＿＿＿＿＿＿＿＿＿＿
3. （水質などを）汚染する　＿＿＿＿＿＿＿＿＿＿＿＿＿
4. 有毒物質　　　　　　＿＿＿＿＿＿＿＿＿＿＿＿＿
5. 排気ガス　　　　　　＿＿＿＿＿＿＿＿＿＿＿＿＿
6. 二酸化炭素　　　　　＿＿＿＿＿＿＿＿＿＿＿＿＿
7. ダイオキシン　　　　＿＿＿＿＿＿＿＿＿＿＿＿＿
8. フロンガス　　　　　＿＿＿＿＿＿＿＿＿＿＿＿＿
9. 環境にやさしい　　　＿＿＿＿＿＿＿＿＿＿＿＿＿
10. 洗剤　　　　　　　　＿＿＿＿＿＿＿＿＿＿＿＿＿

EXERCISES

次の日本語の文を英語に直しなさい。

> **表現のポイント**　☞①
> never before, at no other time in historyなどの否定詞を含む副詞句を文頭において比較級構文を作る場合，主節で完了時制を用いるが，その際主語と助動詞が倒置される点に注意。このような否定副詞句文頭型の構文は，以下に示すような具体主語型のものに比べて，強意的な効果がある。
>
> ①を具体主語を用いてrewriteした例：The earth is more polluted today than ever before.

1. 現代ほど天然資源を大量に消費している時代はかつてなかった。いずれそのツケが回ってくるというはまず間違いないところである。
   ▶ 「天然資源」natural resources 　「～のツケが回る」have to pay the price for～

2. 有史以来，現代ほど大気中の二酸化炭素の濃度が上がった時代はかつてなかった。このままいくと，温室効果がいよいよ大きくなって地球の生態系全体に深刻な影響を及ぼすと考えられている。
   ▶ 「有史以来」In no other time in recorded history で文を始める。「温室効果」greenhouse effect 　「生態系」ecological system

3. かつてなかったほどむごたらしく自然を破壊している現代において，'環境にやさしい' という言葉が脚光を浴びているのは皮肉な事だ。
   ▶ 「むごたらしく」cruelly 　「脚光を浴びる」attract attention 　「皮肉な」ironical

---

表現のポイント　☞②
英語ではnothing, no one, no countryなどの '０要素' を主語にする構文がよく用いられる。日本語にはない構文であるため，日本人学習者にとっては習得の難しい表現形式の一つ。このような '０要素' 主語構文を適切に使う事で，人称主語などの具体主語構文とのcontrastがでて，英作文のメリハリがつく効果がある。

---

4. 生活の様々な面でどっぷりと石油に依存している現代人にとって，石油なしの生活を想像することほど困難な事はないであろう。
   ▶ 「依存する」depend

5. 現代において，他の何物にもまして重要な事は自然環境を保全することに全力をあげることだろう。
   ▶ 「自然環境」natural surroundings 　「保全する」preserve

LET'S TRY !

A ①にならって，'Never before' ではじまる10 words以上の英文を書いてみましょう。

B 'What we can do to stop the environmental pollution getting worse' というタイトルで100 words程度の英文を書いてみましょう。

UNIT 15

My view of marriage

◆代名詞

MODEL PASSAGE   *first-person narrative*

以下の文章をCDで聴いてみましょう。また①〜④の英文に注意しながら、繰り返し音読してみましょう。

 Maya is in her final year at college in Tokyo. Just like other final-year college students, her greatest concern is job hunting. She's applied to a cosmetics company which is doing good business throughout the country. After passing the primary test a few days ago, today she had an interview at the head office of the company in Shinagawa. It was exhausting. Now, on her way back home, Maya reflects on the interviewers' questions and her answers to them. Her thoughts focus on the question of marriage.

 As I'd expected, they asked me, "Miss Sagawa, would you mind if you were transferred to different places every few years?" "I wouldn't mind at all," I answered, "I like moving. Going to new places and mixing with new people would broaden my horizons, I suppose." They also asked me, "Miss Sagawa, if we hire you, we'd like you to work for us for at least ten years. Can you stay with us even when you're married?" ①**I couldn't give an immediate answer because getting married was something I hadn't thought much about,** but I knew saying nothing would be disadvantageous, so I said yes.

Once I start working, I hope to continue as long as I can. If I was forced to choose between marriage or work, I'd certainly take work. I don't think marriage and work ever go hand in hand. ②**It's what happened to my family that makes me think that way.** Both my parents worked outside the home: my father was a car salesman, and my mother was a nurse. They were both so hardworking that they had very little time to spend together. My father was always complaining that no one did any housework in our family. Finally, they got divorced. Since then I've been living with my mother.

I know how expensive it was for them to bring me up. ③**It cost them a fortune to give me a good education**; they sent me to a private high school and now I'm at a private college with their financial help. Besides, when I was at high school they paid for me to learn the piano, dancing, and painting. ④**This made me realize how much money it takes to raise a child.** From a financial point of view, having a family doesn't seem to pay at all. People may say I'm too practical, but I don't want to ask for financial trouble by having children. Anyway, I'm not the family type, so I'll be happier staying single for the rest of my life.

There's another reason, too. There's a new labor law telling employers to treat men and women as equals in the workplace. This means that it's not just men who are sent to other branches; now women may be transferred to a series of different places, which was unusual before. This will make it harder for working women to settle in one place and have a family. I'm afraid fewer and fewer women will be family-oriented.

KEY CLAUSES

以下の日本語は，MODEL PASSAGEの重要構文①～④の和訳です。本文を見ずに，この日本語から元の英文を作り上げる練習をしてみましょう。

① すぐには答えることができませんでした。というのも結婚ということはあまり考えたことがなかったからです。

② 私がそういう風に考えるのは，私の家族の身の上に起こったことが原因なのです。

③ 両親にとっては，私に良い教育を受けさせるのにひと財産使い果たすぐらいのお金がかかったのです。

④ このことで私は，子供ひとり育てるのにどれほどのお金がかかるかよくわかりました。

WORDS & PHRASES

次の日本語の意味に相当する英語を，MODEL PASSAGEの中から抜き出し，書き取ってみましょう。

1. 就職活動　　　　　＿＿＿＿＿＿＿＿＿＿＿＿＿＿
2. 化粧品会社　　　　＿＿＿＿＿＿＿＿＿＿＿＿＿＿
3. 一次試験　　　　　＿＿＿＿＿＿＿＿＿＿＿＿＿＿
4. 視野を広げる　　　＿＿＿＿＿＿＿＿＿＿＿＿＿＿
5. 不利な　　　　　　＿＿＿＿＿＿＿＿＿＿＿＿＿＿
6. 勤勉な　　　　　　＿＿＿＿＿＿＿＿＿＿＿＿＿＿
7. ひと財産　　　　　＿＿＿＿＿＿＿＿＿＿＿＿＿＿
8. 打算的な（割りきった）　＿＿＿＿＿＿＿＿＿＿＿＿
9. 家庭的タイプ（の人物）　＿＿＿＿＿＿＿＿＿＿＿＿
10. マイホーム志向の　＿＿＿＿＿＿＿＿＿＿＿＿＿＿

EXERCISES

次の日本語の文を英語に直しなさい。

> 表現のポイント ☞①
> 例えば，「北海道一人旅なんてのはやってみたいことですね。」の英訳としては
> １）I want to travel around Hokkaido by myselfでもよいが，代名詞のsomethingを使って２）Traveling around Hokkaido by myself is something I want to doでも可。
> ２）のようなX is something S＋Vの構造では，Xが文頭にあるために，１）の場合よりも，Xが強調される文体的効果がある。

1. 職場で男性がいつも女性にあれこれ指図してばかりというのは私にとっては納得がいかないことなのです。
   ▶「あれこれ指図して」tell someone what to do 　「納得がいかない」be unhappy with～

2. 私は家庭向きの人間じゃありません。毎日家事と子供の世話に追われるというのは耐えられません。
   ▶「に追われる」spend every day～ing

> 表現のポイント ☞②
> いわゆる分裂文（cleft sentence）の構造で，It is X that S＋Vの形を使うことでXを意味的に強調することができる。

3. 「Johnは一生結婚なんかしないといってるけど。」「Johnがそういう風に考えるのは両親が離婚したせいなんです。」
   ▶「一生結婚なんかしない」「一生独身のままでいる」と考える。

4. その会社を受けてみようという気になったきっかけは三上先生が私にしてくださったお話でした。
   ▶「という気になったきっかけ」make one decide to doの形が使える。

> 表現のポイント ☞③
> 形式語としてのitを使ってIt～to Vの形でitがto V以下を受ける構文ができあがる。

5. 彼女にフランス料理のフルコースをご馳走してやったらひと財産ふっとんでしまったよ。おかげで今週は文無しだよ。
   ▶「フランス料理のフルコース」a full-course French dinner　「ご馳走する」treat

6. 自分が本当はどういう仕事に向いているかかがわかるまでずいぶん時間がかかりました。
   ▶「向いている」仕事が主語 be suitable for　ひとが主語 be fit for

> 表現のポイント　☞④
> 前のsentence(s)　全体，もしくは前のsentenceの内容の一部を指示代名詞のthisやthatで受け，それを主語とした構文を作ることができる。

7. そのことで私は，外国人が日本で働くということがどういうことなのかよくわかるようになりました。

8. そのことによって，私は女性にとって主婦とOLを両立させることの難しさがわかりました。
   ▶「主婦とOLを両立させる」「主婦であって同時に勤め人(office worker)であること」と考える。

— LET'S TRY！—

A ①にならって 'X is something S＋V' の構文を使って10 words以上の英文を書いてみましょう。

B 'It cost someone a fortune to V' の構文を使って15 words以上の英文を書いてみましょう。

Is Japan an international society?

UNIT 16

◆進行形

MODEL PASSAGE *dialogue*

以下の文章をCDで聴いてみましょう。また①～⑤の英文に注意しながら、繰り返し音読してみましょう。

Emiko, a Japanese girl, and Alex, a student from Australia, are studying at the same university in Japan. One day, they get into conversation about how 'international' Japan is. Emiko feels that Japan is becoming more international, because more Japanese people are going abroad and learning English. Alex disagrees; he rejects the term 'internationalization', and argues that the number of people of different nationalities living in a place is a better criterion of how international that place is.

Emiko: Hi, Alex. I called you yesterday but you must've been out.

Alex: Hi, Emiko. Yes, I had to go down to the travel agent. ①**I was trying to book an air ticket back to Australia for the summer vacation.**

Emiko: Did you manage it?

Alex: No, all the flights are fully booked. But I put my name on the waiting list for a cancellation, so I hope I'll be getting a call from the travel agent before long.

Emiko: All the flights are full? ②**I can't believe how many people are going abroad these days.** ③**It shows you how international Japan is becoming.**

Alex: What do you mean by 'international'?

Emiko: ④**Well, more Japanese are going abroad, and more of them can speak foreign languages like English.** And more tourists from abroad are coming to Japan. It's all part of *kokusaika*—the internationalization of Japan.

Alex: You may be right about more Japanese going abroad, but that doesn't make Japan more 'international,' whatever that means. And there's no such word as 'internationalization'.

Emiko: Isn't there?

Alex: Well, it's not widely used, anyway. I've heard 'international' used to mean the mixing of different nationalities in one place. For example: 'Paris is a very international city—there are people from every part of the world living there.'

Emiko: I see.

Alex: And I suppose it could even mean the use of common standards in different countries. Like the same road signs being used throughout the world, or the same systems of measurement.

Emiko: Well, there are a lot more foreign businesses setting up here in Japan.

Alex: I think that's what's called globalization, rather than internationalization. A small number of huge multinational companies are spreading throughout the world. For example, you can get the same hamburgers in almost every big city in the world.

Emiko: ⑤**Anyway, what I'm talking about is that the Japanese are becoming more internationally-minded, less insular.**

Alex: That could be true, but I'm not sure. I'm still seen as a gaijin wherever I go. This city would be more 'international' if there were more people from different countries living here.

Emiko: But I often see foreigners here.

Alex: No, I mean like New York or London, where out of any ten people walking down the street, over half will probably turn out to be foreigners. In that environment you simply forget about nationality and start treating people as individuals.

Emiko: So one can tell how 'international' a particular place is by seeing how many foreigners live there. Is that what you mean?

Alex: That's right. I think it's a much better criterion than, say, how many people are going abroad.

KEY CLAUSES

以下の日本語は，MODEL PASSAGEの重要構文①〜⑤の和訳です。本文を見ずに，この日本語から元の英文を作り上げる練習をしてみましょう。

① 夏休みにオーストラリアに帰るんでその航空券を予約しようとしたんだよ。

② 最近どれほど多くの人々が海外に出かけているかはちょっと信じられないくらいだわ。

③ それで日本がどれほど国際化してきたかがわかるわ。

④ えーとそれは，海外に出かける日本人が増えてきているし，英語とかの外国語を話せる日本人の数も増えてるしね。

⑤ とにかく，私が今話しているのは日本人がどんどん国際的な視野を持つようになってきて，島国根性が薄れてきているということなのよ。

WORDS & PHRASES

次の日本語の意味に相当する英語を，MODEL PASSAGEの中から抜き出し，書き取ってみましょう。

1. 予約する　　　　　　　　　_____
2. キャンセル待ちのリスト　　_____
3. 国際都市　　　　　　　　　_____
4. 共通のものさし　　　　　　_____
5. 外資系の会社　　　　　　　_____
6. 地球規模化　　　　　　　　_____
7. バーガー　　　　　　　　　_____
8. 国際的視野を持った　　　　_____
9. 国籍　　　　　　　　　　　_____
10. （判断の）基準　　　　　　_____

EXERCISES

次の日本語の文を英語に直しなさい。

> 表現のポイント
> 英語の進行形（Progressive Form）は基本的には，一時的に進行している事柄にスポットライトをあてるはたらきがある。ただしその一時性（temporariness）は例えば，12月3日の10時現在のような狭い意味での一時性（cf. John is watching TV at home）を表す場合と，例えば1990年代以降の最近の傾向（cf. These days, more and more Japanese are going abroad.）などのように，ゆるやかな意味での一時性がある。

1. 昨日君がファックスをよこしてきた時，僕は「大阪はどの程度国際化しているか」という本を読んでたところだった。
   ▶「ファックスをよこす」send someone a fax

2. 最近どのくらいの数の若者が髪を染めているか信じられないくらいだよ。世の中にはこれを，日本人であることがいやになってきていることの現れだと見る人もいるよ。
   ▶「髪を染める」dye one's hair

3. その数字を見ればその国がどのくらい民族主義的，軍国主義的になってきているかわかる。
   ▶「民族主義的，軍国主義的」nationalistic and militaristic

4. 最近日本に来ている外国人の犯罪がやたらと多くなってきているのは事実だ。
   ▶「犯罪を犯す」commit a crime

5. 最近夏休みや春休みを利用して海外にホームステイする若者がとても多いのですが，そのことで彼らが国際的になっていると思いますか。
   ▶「利用して」for 「そのことで〜」はhelp someone to doの構文が使える。

6. 海外からの観光客が増えているというのはいいことことだと思うけど，彼らがどの程度日本人と日本文化を理解しているかとなるとよくわからないね。
   ▶「日本文化」Japanese culture

7. 最初はよくわからないといっていたけれど，最近うちのクラスの学生も 'globalization' の正確な意味と用法がだんだんわかるようになってきているようだ。
   ▶「だんだんわかるようになってきている」be beginning to understand

— LET'S TRY !

A 'become' を進行形で使って10 words以上の英文を書いてみましょう。

B 'What I hope to get from traveling abroad' というタイトルで100 words程度の英文を書いてみましょう。

Job prospects for college students

UNIT **17**

◆文修飾副詞

MODEL PASSAGE   *third-person essay*

以下の文章をCDで聴いてみましょう。また①〜⑤の英文に注意しながら、繰り返し音読してみましょう。

①**Unfortunately, the Japanese economy has been slowing down in recent years, and this has adversely affected the job prospects of college students.** Corporations, large and small, are being forced to restructure in order to survive, and this means they have to sack or lay off many 'unimportant' employees. Under these circumstances, employers are very reluctant to hire unskilled people fresh from college. Consequently, fewer college graduates are finding work.

②**Not surprisingly, quite a few students give up the idea of working for someone else, and decide to start a small business of their own.** Some are successful, but the number is hopelessly small. ③**Clearly, what is behind this unhappy situation is the way the Japanese traditionally think of work.** For the average Japanese, working means working for someone, and self employment isn't necessarily considered an ideal way of obtaining high social status, which is often enjoyed by those working for big companies.

④**Interestingly enough, more and more people nowadays are hopping from one part-time job to another, rather than get a permanent job at a company, and many of them are college graduates.** They say they enjoy their jobs because they are free from all the obligations that full-time workers are supposed to feel towards their companies. ⑤**This new type of worker is undoubtedly becoming more common in present-day Japan.**

KEY CLAUSES

以下の日本語は，MODEL PASSAGEの重要構文①〜⑤の和訳です。本文を見ずに，この日本語から元の英文を作り上げる練習をしてみましょう。

① 不幸なことに日本経済は近年落ち込んできており，そのことが大学生の就職状況に悪影響を与えるようになってきた。

② かなりの数の学生がどこかに勤めるという考えをやめて，自分でベンチャービジネスを始めようと決意しているのは驚くにはあたらない。

③ 明らかに，この不幸な状況の背景としてあるのは日本人の仕事に対する昔からの考えである。

④ 興味深いのは，最近では一つの会社でずっと働くのではなく，次から次にパートの仕事を変えていく人が増えているが，その多くが大卒であるという点だ。

⑤ この種の新しいタイプの労働者が現代の日本で一般的になってきているのは間違いない。

WORDS & PHRASES

次の日本語の意味に相当する英語を，MODEL PASSAGEの中から抜き出し，書き取ってみましょう。

1. 日本経済　　　＿＿＿＿＿＿＿＿＿＿＿＿＿＿＿＿
2. リストラする　＿＿＿＿＿＿＿＿＿＿＿＿＿＿＿＿
3. 解雇する　　　＿＿＿＿＿＿＿＿＿＿＿＿＿＿＿＿
4. 一時解雇する　＿＿＿＿＿＿＿＿＿＿＿＿＿＿＿＿
5. ベンチャービジネス　＿＿＿＿＿＿＿＿＿＿＿＿＿
6. 自営業　　　　＿＿＿＿＿＿＿＿＿＿＿＿＿＿＿＿
7. 社会的地位　　＿＿＿＿＿＿＿＿＿＿＿＿＿＿＿＿
8. 大企業　　　　＿＿＿＿＿＿＿＿＿＿＿＿＿＿＿＿
9. 定職　　　　　＿＿＿＿＿＿＿＿＿＿＿＿＿＿＿＿
10. 義務　　　　　＿＿＿＿＿＿＿＿＿＿＿＿＿＿＿＿

EXERCISES

次の日本語の文を英語に直しなさい。

> **表現のポイント**
> 文修飾副詞（sentence adverb）は，文中の特定の語句を修飾するのではなく，文全体を修飾するはたらきがあり，通例文頭（または文尾）におかれるが，文中に用いられることもある。文修飾副詞は話者の心情，見解，判断など様々な意味を表し，よく使われるのは以下のようなもの。fortunately, unfortunately, luckily, apparently, surprisingly, interestingly enough, clearly, strangely enough, personally, etc.
> 日本語の場合「～は（が）～であるが，これは実に興味深いことだ」「～は（が）～であるが，これは別に驚くにはあたらない」などのように，話者の心情，見解，判断などは文章の中で後置され易いが，そのような日本文を英訳する場合，文修飾副詞を使うと，英語らしい表現になることが多い。

1. 日本の不況はずい分長引いているが，これは不運なことだ。
    ▶「不況」recession

2. 自分の子供を一時的な仕事ではなく定職につかせたいと願う親が多いが，これは別に驚くにはあたらない。
    ▶「一時的な仕事」part-time job 「定職」permanent job

3. 大卒の来年の就職の見とおしが，昨年なみに厳しいものになることは明らかである。
    ▶「就職の見とおし」the job prospects of college graduates

4. 就職活動を始めたとたん，急に態度がまじめになって，身なりもきちんとしてくる学生が多いのはおもしろい現象だ。
    ▶「就職活動」job hunting 「態度がまじめになる」become well-behaved

5. 民間企業の倒産が相次ぐ現在，今後ますます公務員志望の若者が増えていくことは間違いない。
    ▶「民間企業」private corporations 「公務員」government employee

6. あれほど弁護士になりたがっていた水野君が，急に弁護士はいやだと言い出したのは実に奇妙なことだ。
   ▶「弁護士」lawyer

7. わたしは競争率100倍の就職試験を突破できて幸運でした。
   ▶「競争率100倍」100 applicants for each vacancy　「就職試験」employment exam

8. 私は個人的には，安定志向の連中より，リスクを恐れず新しい事に挑戦するタイプの人間が好きです。
   ▶「リスクを恐れず」without being afraid of taking risks

LET'S TRY!

A 'unfortunately' を使って10 words以上の英文を書いてみましょう。

B 'undoubtedly' を使って15 words以上の英文を書いてみましょう。

A problem with Japan's education system UNIT 18

◆ 'when' の２つの用法

MODEL PASSAGE   *third-person essay*

以下の文章をCDで聴いてみましょう。また①〜⑤の英文に注意しながら、繰り返し音読してみましょう。

It is well known that Japanese students work hard before they get into college. Entrance exams, especially those for famous universities, are highly competitive, although these days the situation is beginning to change as the number of 18-year-olds falls. For students, preparing for university entrance exams is perhaps the most time-consuming and exhausting activity of their whole lives; many of them go to *juku* after school to get a head start over their rivals. Before finally getting a place at university, they take hundreds of mock tests; some students fail once or twice at actual exams and have to wait until the following year to try again. ①**So it is not surprising that many feel, when they are finally admitted to the university of their choice, that they've completed the most difficult job of their lives.**

②**Until the age of 18 or 19, when they become college students, many Japanese are very highly motivated learners.** After that, however, their motivation declines sharply, partly because they've spent so much energy studying for the entrance exams that they feel they have very little energy left for further study, and partly because, from the institutional point of view, ③ **higher education in Japan hasn't yet succeeded in offering a scheme that encourages students to learn more enthusiastically than when they were university applicants.**

④**In terms of intellectual development, human beings are more capable of thinking, reasoning and understanding when they are twenty or over than in their teens.** ⑤**It's regrettable that intellectually they are relatively inactive while they are at university, when they ought to be active and creative.** Perhaps Japan's education system has been wasting a good deal of people's time and energy by forcing many of them to work hard at the wrong time, and by letting them rest at the wrong time.

KEY CLAUSES

以下の日本語は，MODEL PASSAGEの重要構文①〜⑤の和訳です。本文を見ずに，この日本語から元の英文を作り上げる練習をしてみましょう。

① したがって，日本の学生は自分の志望大学に最終的に入学した時に，一生のうちで最も困難な仕事をやり終えたという気持ちになっても全く不思議はない。

② 多くの日本人が大学生になる18歳もしくは19歳の年までは，彼らは非常に学習意欲の高い人間なのである。

③ 日本の高等教育は大学受験の時以上に学生に勉強させる仕組みをまだ提供することができていないのである。

④ 知力の発達という観点からすると人間は10代の時よりも，20歳になってからのほうが思考力，推論能力，そして理解力がより高いのである

⑤ 残念なのは，日本の大学生は，本来元気はつらつ，かつ創造的であるべき大学時代に，知的な意味で比較的元気がないという点である。

WORDS & PHRASES

次の日本語の意味に相当する英語を，MODEL PASSAGEの中から抜き出し，書き取ってみましょう。

1. 日本の教育制度　　　　＿＿＿＿＿＿＿＿＿＿＿＿＿＿
2. 競争がきびしい　　　　＿＿＿＿＿＿＿＿＿＿＿＿＿＿
3. 18歳人口　　　　　　　＿＿＿＿＿＿＿＿＿＿＿＿＿＿
4. （まわりに差をつけるために）
　　先んじる　　　　　　＿＿＿＿＿＿＿＿＿＿＿＿＿＿
5. 模擬試験　　　　　　　＿＿＿＿＿＿＿＿＿＿＿＿＿＿
6. 本試　　　　　　　　　＿＿＿＿＿＿＿＿＿＿＿＿＿＿
7. 動機付けの高い学習者　＿＿＿＿＿＿＿＿＿＿＿＿＿＿
8. 高等教育　　　　　　　＿＿＿＿＿＿＿＿＿＿＿＿＿＿
9. 大学受験生　　　　　　＿＿＿＿＿＿＿＿＿＿＿＿＿＿
10. 残念な　　　　　　　　＿＿＿＿＿＿＿＿＿＿＿＿＿＿

EXERCISES

次の日本語の文を英語に直しなさい。

> 表現のポイント　☞①,③,④
> 時を表す副詞節を導くwhenの用法。When節＋主節，あるいは，主節＋when節の形になるが，場合によっては①のようにwhen節が主節の中に挿入的に用いられる時もある。また③のように，比較級がらみで使われる時は接続詞のthanの次にwhen節が直結する構造になる。

1. 佐田君がこのあいだ，大学受験の勉強をしていた時はわれながらよく勉強していたけれど，大学に入った後，頭が働かなくなった，と言っていた。
   ▶「頭が働かない」頭（mind）がidle（or empty）と考える。

2. 日本人の学生の中には，長年の努力のすえに志望大学に合格した時，仕事は終わった，あとは余生だ，と短絡的に考えてしまうものが少なからずいる。
   ▶「あとは余生だ」spend the rest of their lives peacefully　「短絡的にかんがえる」think in a simplistic way

3. 一般的に人間は何か目標がある時の方が，ない時よりも学習動機は高くなる傾向がある。
   ▶「目標」goal , aim, purpose

4. 杉田君は恐ろしく活動的なタイプの人間だ。彼に言わせると，何かに熱中している時の方が全くヒマな時よりも気持ちが安らぐそうだ。
   ▶「気持ちが安らぐ」relax

> 表現のポイント　☞②,⑤
> 副詞節を導くwhenと異なり，関係詞としてのwhenの場合，the age of 18 or 19や，at university（⑤の文脈ではat universityは場所ではなく「大学時代」という意味で用いられている）などのような，時を表す名詞句に直結する形で用いられる。

5. 家庭の主婦の中には50代，60代になって子供が手を離れた時，大学で勉強をし始める人がかなりいる。
   ▶「子供が手を離れた時」「もう子供の面倒を見なくてよい時」と考える。

6. 遊びほうけていたい子供の頃にやれ塾だ，ピアノだ，お習字だと習いごとで子供をしばり込むのはやはりどこか間違っている気がする。
   ▶「お習字」calligraphy 「しばり込む」force～to V

7. Robertは20代の，最も知力が活発だった時になまけていたことを今ひどく後悔している
   ▶「後悔する」regret

LET'S TRY！

A 関係詞としての 'when' を使って10 words以上の英文を書いてみましょう。

B 'How is it possible to make Japanese college students work harder?' というタイトルで100 words程度の英文を書いてみましょう

UNIT 19

High school vs. cram school

◆使役動詞

MODEL PASSAGE *dialogue*

以下の文章をCDで聴いてみましょう。また①〜⑤の英文に注意しながら、繰り返し音読してみましょう。

 Mamoru is a 17-year-old high-school boy. He enjoys life a great deal. He is a member of the school tennis club; he loves tennis, and practices hard. At the same time he's working very hard because he hopes to get into a state university in Tokyo next year. To prepare for the entrance exams, he's going to a juku or cram school every Saturday and Sunday. One day, Mr. Ward, an ALT at Mamoru's high school, asks him about how he's getting on at high school and juku.

Mr. Ward: Hi, Mamoru, how's everything going?
Mamoru: Fine, thank you, Mr. Ward. I'm really enjoying life at the moment.
Mr. Ward: That's good. Mamoru, I understand you're pretty busy on weekends going to *juku*. Could I ask you why you go to *juku*? Are you unhappy with the way your studies are going here at school?
Mamoru: No, I'm happy enough. I find school life here pretty satisfying; my only complaint is that the school rules are too strict. Why do I go to *juku*? The *juku* teachers are experts on university entrance exams; they give me a lot of useful information. They're good teachers, too. ①**They know how to make themselves understood, ②and how to get the students to work efficiently.**
Mr. Ward: You mean the *juku* teachers are much better than the teachers here?
Mamoru: No, I don't. Most of the teachers here are very good; they're enthusiastic and friendly. But sometimes they are very authoritative and domineering; ③**they make us do things we don't want to do, such as getting our hair cut too short.**
Mr. Ward: Mamoru, let me tell you this. Teaching isn't the only thing high school teachers have to do; ④**having the students obey the school rules, for example, is an important part of their job.** I hope you understand this.

Mamoru: Well, what I like best about going to *juku* is that there's a different relationship between teachers and students there. At *juku*, teachers put all their energy into teaching, and students concentrate on learning. Teachers are assessed by their students, and their salary depends on how popular they are with their students.

Mr. Ward: That sounds very business-like, doesn't it? As though *juku* teachers were shop assistants and the students were their customers. I've heard some of them try hard to be good entertainers—always trying to say or do something amusing to increase their popularity with their students. Doesn't that kind of thing happen?

Mamoru: ⑤**Last year a teacher at my juku even bought each of his students an ice-cream to get them to come to his class the following week.**

Mr. Ward: That's funny, and rather sad. So what happened to the teacher?

Mamoru: He was fired in the end. He'd been unpopular for some time, and his students despised him all the more for what he did. But he was an exception. Generally, the students respect the ones who teach well, and good teachers don't try to please the students except through their teaching.

Mr. Ward: Not to change the subject, but you play tennis, Mamoru. Are club activities available at *juku*?

Mamoru: No, they aren't, but that's not what I want from *juku*; all I want from *juku* is an environment where I can work really hard for the entrance exams. Going to high school is good because I can play tennis, and that lets me get rid of all the frustration that builds up when I'm working. That's one way high school is better than *juku*, I suppose.

Mr. Ward: So you're enjoying the advantages of both high school and *juku*, aren't you?

Mamoru: Yes, you're right, Mr. Ward.

KEY CLAUSES

以下の日本語は，MODEL PASSAGEの重要構文①〜⑤の和訳です。本文を見ずに，この日本語から元の英文を作り上げる練習をしてみましょう。

① 彼らは（塾の先生は）自分が伝えたいことをきちんと相手に伝えるノウハウを持っています。

② それに（塾の先生は），どうすれば学生に効率的な学習指導ができるかも（わかっています）。

③ 学校の教師は，例えば，極端に髪の毛を短くさせたりして，私達がやりたがらないことを無理やりやらせようとします。

④ 例えば学生に校則を守らせるのは，学校の教師の仕事の重要な部分なのです。

⑤ 去年，私が通っている塾の教師が，その次の週もちゃんと授業に来てもらいたいということで，学生のひとりひとりにアイスクリームを買って与えたということがありました。

WORDS & PHRASES

次の日本語の意味に相当する英語を，MODEL PASSAGEの中から抜き出し，書き取ってみましょう。

1. 校則　　　　　　　_____
2. プロ（専門家）　　_____
3. 効率よく　　　　　_____
4. 熱心な　　　　　　_____
5. 権威主義的　　　　_____
6. いばりちらす　　　_____
7. 事務的な　　　　　_____
8. 首になる　　　　　_____
9. 軽蔑する　　　　　_____
10. クラブ活動　　　　_____

EXERCISES

次の日本語の文を英語に直しなさい。

> **表現のポイント ☞①**
> make oneself understoodで，相手に自分の言いたいことを伝える，わからせるという意味になる。この動詞句の場合，oneselfの次に原形のunderstandではなく過去分詞であるunderstoodが来る点に注意。このoneself understoodで自分が理解されという受動の意味が成立する。

1. 自分の言いたいことを相手にきちんと伝えるのは意外に難しいものだ。
    ▶「意外に難しい」「一般に思われているより難しい」と考える。

> **表現のポイント ☞②**
> get someone to do〜は，一般的に，目的語にあたる人物に何事かを強制してやらせるということではなく，主として言葉での説得によってある行動をとらせるという意味で用いられることが多い。

2. うちの大学の学生がまじめに勉強するようにしむけるのは並大抵のことじゃない。
    ▶「まじめに勉強する」work hard

3. 加藤君はサークルで忙しすぎて最近ほとんど僕のゼミに出てこないね。このままじゃ卒業が危ないので，君が何とか説得して来させてくれないか。
    ▶「ゼミ」seminar

> **表現のポイント ☞③**
> make someone do〜は目的語にあたる人物などの気持ち，意向などを無視して，無理やり何かをさせるという強制的な意味になる。

4. むりやり子供に塾に行かせようとしてもむだですよ。子供が自分でその気になるまで待った方が利口だと思います。
    ▶「利口」wise

5. 林田先生はわかりやすい授業をするのはいいんだけれど，時々無理に英語で何かを言わせようとするところがきらいだ。
    ▶「〜はいいんだけれど」it's good that S＋V, but〜の構文が使える。

表現のポイント　☞④

have someone do～は，一般的に，目的語にあたる人物の願望の有無にかかわらず，主語にあたる目上の人物（教師，上司，親など）が目下の人物（生徒，部下，子供）に何かをさせるという意味で使われる。

6. 日本では，子供達に教室の掃除をさせるのも教育の重要な一環であるという考え方が一般的である。
   ▶「教室を掃除する」clean the classroom　「一環」part

7. 学生にある程度の長さの英文を暗誦させるのは，学生に英語力をつける上で非常に効果的だと思います。
   ▶「ある程度の長さの」of some length

LET'S TRY!

A 'get (got) someone to do something' の構文を使って10 words以上の英文を書いてみましょう。

B 'make (made) someone do～' の構文を使って15 words程度の英文を書いてみましょう。

UNIT 20

Why are cars so important?

◆総合演習

MODEL PASSAGE   *dialogue*

以下の文章をCDで聴いてみましょう。また①〜④の英文に注意しながら、繰り返し音読してみましょう。

　Hideo is a businessman in his late twenties; he runs an Internet company in Yokohama. Everything's going well for him: his company is successful; he has an attractive girlfriend; and he has recently bought a brand new car. He loves cars—in fact, he sometimes feels more in love with his new car than with his girlfriend. James, who's a year or so younger, is from Scotland. He works for a well-known computer company. Hideo and James first met through work several years ago, and have kept in touch with each other since. One day, they relax after a business meeting at James' office.

James: Hideo, I hear you bought a new car recently. What happened to the old one?

Hideo: I traded it in for a new one.

James: I can't believe it! The one you had was a new Mitsubishi, wasn't it? You only got it a year or so ago.

Hideo: Well, it was a really good car, but I felt really excited when I saw the latest Rover model. I fell in love with it at first sight. It was four million yen, a bit expensive, but I bought it anyway.

James: ①**Hideo, how many cars did you have before the Rover?**

Hideo: **Four, I guess.**

James: Wow! And you love your new 'sweetheart' very much?

Hideo: Oh, yes. The specs are excellent; its 200-hp DOHC engine is really powerful and smooth. I go to and from work in that car, and almost every weekend I go for a drive in it with my girlfriend.

James: So this brand new car is now part of your everyday life?

Hideo: Yes, you could say that. I love it so much that I sometimes feel it's an extension of my body. I'm doing my best to keep it in immaculate condition. I wash and wax it whenever I have time.

James: Seems to me that most Japanese are just like you—they take very good care of their cars. ②**They can't stand the smallest dent or scratch on them.**

Hideo: If my car got even a tiny, almost imperceptible dent in it, I'd get it fixed straight away, no matter how much it cost.

James: I don't understand why you're so fussy about your car. I have a car myself, a seven-year-old Toyota, but a car is just another possession like a TV set or a tape recorder. As long as my car keeps going, and gets me from one place to another, I'm happy with it. It has some scratches and a few dents, but I don't care; it runs perfectly well with them, so I've done nothing about them. And it's dirty; the last time I washed it was about six months ago. ③**But I just don't care; it goes very well, and that's what counts.**

Hideo: That's a British way of thinking, a very practical one. It reminds me of something that happened on my trip to Britain three years ago. I was surprised when a friend of mine gave me a lift in his car; there were so many empty cans and bottles scattered around on the seats and the floor that there was hardly any room to sit, and it seemed to me the car hadn't been cleaned for years. But my friend didn't mind this at all; he said he liked his car because it hardly ever broke down.

James: That doesn't surprise me. Plenty of British people are just like that. And you must have noticed how many people were driving small or medium-sized cars over there.

Hideo: Right, a lot of people were driving Nissan Micras; it's a very popular 1000-cc car in Britain.

James: It shows that people don't see their cars as status symbols in Britain; even university professors and company executives are perfectly happy driving small cars like the one you mentioned. In the US, famous university professors, for example, wouldn't want a small car, and the same applies in Japan.

Hideo: Perhaps Americans tend to think that the car you own reflects how successful you are, and quite a few Japanese, including me, feel more or less the same way.

James: To a lot of British people, having a big flashy car would seem like boasting.

Hideo: ④**Anyway, it's interesting to see how different attitudes toward cars reflect different cultures.**

KEY CLAUSES

以下の日本語は，MODEL PASSAGEの重要構文①~④の和訳です。本文を見ずに，この日本語から元の英文を作り上げる練習をしてみましょう。

① 「英雄，そのローバーで何台目になるんだい。」「5台目だよ。」

② 日本人は自分の車の，どんな小さなへこみや傷でもがまんできないんだ。

③ でも僕は全然気にしないね。とにかくよく走ってくれるし，それが大事なんだよ。

④ ともあれ，車に対する考え方がそれぞれ違う文化を反映しているのを知るのはおもしろいね。

WORDS & PHRASES

次の日本語の意味に相当する英語を，MODEL PASSAGEの中から抜き出し，書き取ってみましょう。

1. 下取りに出す　　　　　　　＿＿＿＿＿＿＿＿＿＿＿＿＿＿
2. スペック（仕様）　　　　　＿＿＿＿＿＿＿＿＿＿＿＿＿＿
3. 無傷でピカピカの　　　　　＿＿＿＿＿＿＿＿＿＿＿＿＿＿
4. へこみ　　　　　　　　　　＿＿＿＿＿＿＿＿＿＿＿＿＿＿
5. 擦り傷　　　　　　　　　　＿＿＿＿＿＿＿＿＿＿＿＿＿＿
6. 感知できない　　　　　　　＿＿＿＿＿＿＿＿＿＿＿＿＿＿
7. イギリス的ものの考え方　　＿＿＿＿＿＿＿＿＿＿＿＿＿＿
8. 中型車　　　　　　　　　　＿＿＿＿＿＿＿＿＿＿＿＿＿＿
9. 地位の象徴　　　　　　　　＿＿＿＿＿＿＿＿＿＿＿＿＿＿
10. 会社の重役　　　　　　　　＿＿＿＿＿＿＿＿＿＿＿＿＿＿

EXERCISES

次の日本語の文を英語に直しなさい。

> **表現のポイント ☞①**
> 日本語の「何台目，何番めですか」という序数的なquestionを英語にする時は「それ以前に何台あったか，その人以前に何人いたか」という風に表す。

1. 「George，今度の新しいガールフレンドは何人目ですか。」「4人目だよ。」

2. 「吉田君，うちの会社の社長は何代目か知っているかい。」「確か6代目ですよ。」
   ▶「社長」president

> **表現のポイント ☞②**
> 最上級表現を適切に使うことで，「どんな～でも」という譲歩的意味を簡潔な表現で書くことができる。

3. どんな大きな乗用車でも12人はちょっと無理です。

4. どんなに燃費のいい車でも，リッター50キロはちょっと無理です。
   ▶「燃費のいい」fuel-efficient

> **表現のポイント ☞③**
> 関係詞のwhatを，X is what～のように補語節を導くものとして，あるいはwhat S＋V is Xのように主語節を導くものとして使用することで，日本語の名詞的表現（望み，希望，重要なこと）を端的な節構造で表すことができる。

5. 私がずっと欲しいと思っていたのは強力馬力の四駆車です。
   ▶「四駆車」four-wheel drive car

6. このボルボの新車はこのスペックで350万ですか。私の希望にぴったりですよ。
   ▶「ボルボ」Volvo

UNIT 20

> 表現のポイント 👉 ④
> 英語の不定詞構造であるto see wh節は比較的頻度の高い構文で，日本語の体言がらみの構造（例：仕事ぶりを見るために: to see how hard someone's working, 人柄を知るために: to see what someone is like）を簡潔に表すことができる。

7. 買い手が，これから買おうとする車がどの程度安全性が高いかを確かめようとするのは当然だよ。
   ▶ 「買い手」customers　Customers have every reason to Vの構文が使える。

8. 明日社長が，この浜の町支店の営業ぶりを視察に来るらしいよ。
   ▶ 「営業ぶり」「どのくらいよくやっているか」と考える

LET'S TRY !

A 'see how S + V' の構文を使って10 words以上の英文を書いてみましょう。

B 'Could we do without cars?' というタイトルで100 words程度の英文を書いてみましょう。

本書にはカセットテープ(別売)があります

Read Better to Write Better
―モデル英文からのライティング―

2002年1月20日　初版発行
2024年2月20日　重版発行

著　者　　富　岡　龍　明
　　　　　James　　Hill
発行者　　福　岡　正　人
発行所　　株式会社　金　星　堂
（〒101-0051）東京都千代田区神田神保町 3-21
Tel. 営業部 (03)3263-3828　編集部 (03)3263-3997　Fax. (03)3263-0716
E-mail: 営業部 text@kinsei-do.co.jp

印刷所／加藤文明社　製本所／松島製本　1-8-3757
落丁・乱丁本はお取り替えいたします

ISBN978-4-7647-3757-0　C1082